Praise for *Play Smart*

"*Play Smart* is a well-researched book and a game-changer for young professional women. The actionable solutions and strategies on how to navigate obstacles in a male-dominated workplace are a breath of fresh air, and the personal anecdotes make it a compelling read for anyone looking to succeed in their career."

Kimberly Davis, Head of Compliance,
Investment Company –
Large Academic Endowment

"*Play Smart* offers invaluable strategies for women in male-dominated workplaces while providing men with crucial insights into workplace challenges. As a legal advocate, 'Play Smart' is a must-read for all seeking workplace equity!"

Rodney Acker, Of Counsel, Norton Rose Fulbright,
US LLP; Past President: American
College of Trial Lawyers

"*Play Smart* delivers a compelling blend of heartfelt advice and hard-hitting strategies for women navigating male-dominated environments in any field of work. As a vital contribution to the national dialogue on workplace gender equality, it offers a unique and essential perspective on achieving professional excellence. Additionally, it stands as an invaluable resource for men, providing deep insights into the challenges faced by their female colleagues and equipping them to become more effective allies in fostering a more inclusive and equitable work environment."

Dr. Chitra Fine, MD, Anesthesiology (retired 2024)

"*Play Smart*, the highly anticipated second installment in the 'Sandbox Series,' is a valuable resource for young professionals, especially women, seeking to thrive in the workplace. It offers practical advice and strategies to navigate workplace challenges, with a focus on both male- and female-dominated environments. Men equally benefit from reading this book, gaining deep insights into the challenges faced by female colleagues, and learning how to become better allies. Whether aiming to excel professionally to help navigate difficult territory with confidence or promote workplace equality, *Play Smart* is an essential guide for success."

Joel L. Ross, Former General Counsel of Trammell Crow Company and Retired Partner of Vinson & Elkins LLP

"As a young woman working in a male dominated industry, I wholeheartedly encourage others in my position to not only read this book but use it as a guide throughout their careers. *Play Smart* offers tactical tips and examples for how to manage certain tricky situations in the workplace, small or large. This thoughtful guide really helped me anticipate when tough situations might be coming and how to adapt without compromising my own opportunities. While it may be an uphill battle, *Play Smart* gave me comfort that many women face these same hurdles and equipped me with various strategies to overcome them."

Mia Blackman, Vice President, Crow Holdings Capital

"*Play Smart* is as an important resource for today's working women—the ideal follow-up to the author's initial work, *Play Nice*. Together, these two books offer comprehensive guide to ensure women have a clear understanding of what constitutes inappropriate behavior in the workplace, including sexual harassment, the importance of setting personal boundaries about what we will and will not tolerate, and key advice on how to be treated in a professional, respectful way that allows us to contribute and succeed in our chosen workplace. What I appreciated the most about *Play Smart* is its clear emphasis on the importance of personal performance. The book highlights that respect in the workplace begins with excelling in the tasks assigned to us, a fundamental principle that every woman can and should adopt. *Play Smart* effectively illustrates how focusing on personal performance can pave the way for professional success and respect in the workplace."

Shauna King, Chief Transformation Officer, PepsiCo (retired)/Vice President Finance and Business Operations, Yale University (retired)

THE SANDBOX SERIES
PLAY SMART
Playground Strategies for Success in a Male-Dominated Workplace

BRIGITTE GAWENDA KIMICHIK, JD

Copyright © 2024 by Brigitte Gawenda Kimichik.

All rights reserved. No part of this book may be used or reproduced in any manner without written permission except in the case of brief quotations embodied in critical articles or reviews. The Information and advice presented in this book are limited in scope and general in nature and do not consider developments that may have taken place after the book's composition and publication. This book contains the opinions and ideas of its author. This book is not intended to provide legal, psychological, or other professional services to the reader and does not take the place of consultation with an appropriate professional.

Play Smart – Playground Strategies for Success in a Male-Dominated Workplace

For information: The Sandbox Series LLC, 6228 Tulip Lane, Dallas, Texas 75230, (214) 893-0634, www.thesandboxseries.com.
Name: Kimichik, Brigitte Gawenda, author.
Title: Play Smart – Playground Strategies for Success in a Male-Dominated Workplace
Description: Dallas, Texas: *The Sandbox Series LLC* | Series:
THE SANDBOX SERIES
THE SANDBOX SERIES is a registered trademark of The Sandbox Series LLC

Subjects:
Business & Money | Women in Business | Workplace Culture | Gender Discrimination
Business & Money | Women in Business | Motivation & Self Improvement
Self-Help | Success at Work

Identifiers:
ISBN 979-8-9909126-1-8 (paperback)
ISBN 979-8-9909126-2-5 (e-book)

For more information or to contact the author (including for bulk purchases at a discount), please go to www.TheSandboxSeries.com.

Dedication

To the fearless trailblazers who have shattered glass ceilings in male-dominated industries, to the relentless barrier-breakers who refuse to be held back, and to the champions of equality who understand the power of supporting and empowering women in the workplace. May this book ignite a fire within you, guiding you towards your dreams and empowering you to conquer any challenge in your chosen field.

Contents

Author's Note	xvii
Introduction	**1**
The False Perception of Equal Opportunity	1
We Have Not Come Far Enough	7
The Goal of Play Smart	9
The Meaning of the Sandbox on the Playground of the Work Environment	11
Being Proactive is Key	12

Chapter 1
Understanding The Obstacles and Potential Barriers to Career Progression — 15

> **Rule No. 1: Evaluate and Understand Obstacles**

Evaluate and Understand the Risks before you enter the Playground, this is vital.	15
— Breaking The Glass Ceiling—It is Not a Myth	17
— Combating Unconscious or Implicit Bias and Gender Discrimination	22
— Dealing with Sexism, Discrimination, and Sexual Harassment	29
— The Boys' Club—Barrier or Opportunity?	31
— Lack of Mentors and Sponsors for Career Progression	31
— Battling Self Doubt; Insecurities; and Lack of Confidence—Why Women Fail to Toot Their Horn	32
— Lack of Transparency; Unequal Pay	34
— The Maternity Leave Dilemma	34
— Lack of Convenient Childcare—Don't Hang Up Your Career	36

Chapter 2
The Importance of Self-Help in Addressing Obstacles   38

> **Rule No. 2: Tackle Obstacles Play by Play**

The Importance of Self-Help Measures in Addressing Obstacles   38
- Establish Your Boundaries   39
- Taking Action Builds Confidence   40
- Foster Dialogue for Support   40
- Promote a Culture of Accountability   41
- Foster Corrective Action   41

Chapter 3
Our Playground Rules for Success   43

> **Rule No. 3: Learn the Rules for Success**

Learn the Rules of the Sandbox; Be Ready and Prepared to Play, Take Your Job Seriously, Be Invested in Your Job   43
- Understand Your Company's Business, Industry and Customers   44

Personal Development. Building Credibility:
- Be a Team Player; Roll Up Your Sleeves; Dig In; Be Flexible   45
- Don't Skip Meetings   47
- Pay Attention and Take Notes   48
- Understand Your Assignments, Set Expectations, and Ask for Feedback   48
- Learn How to Delegate for Success as Appropriate   49
- Don't Give Anyone a Reason to Challenge Your Abilities; Be Prepared and Produce Quality Work Product   49
- Work Hard   50
- Knowledge is Power; Do Your Research   51
- Learn From Prior Transactions   51
- Learn How to Add Value, Foster Respect, Confidence and Reliability   52
- Be True to Your Word; Be Reliable; Follow Through with Commitments   53
- Managing Deadlines and Expectations—Don't Be Afraid to Say "No" Nicely   54

Contents

- Address Disagreements Head On — 56
- Acknowledging You Made a Mistake — 56
- Welcome Constructive Feedback — 57
- Learn From the Good and the Bad — 58
- Keep a Positive Attitude — 58
- Focus on the Positives if your Project Outcome Fails — 59
- Keep Communications Professional—Limit Personal Information — 59
- Be Informative, Succinct, and Direct — 59
- Negotiating Skills and Conflict Resolution — 60
- Be Organized and Professional — 61
- Your Office or Workspace — 62
- Your Work Product — 63
- Step Out of Your Comfort Zone—If You Are Not Busy, Ask for Work — 63
- Work Outside Your Section or Group — 64
- Challenge Your Abilities, Volunteer for Difficult Tasks — 64
- Manage Your Position on the Team—Ask for What You Want—Set Project-Based Goals — 65
- Take on More Responsibility; Take on Leadership Roles — 65
- Develop Goals for Your Future — 66

Chapter 4
Important Do's and Don'ts for The Sandbox — 68

> **Rule No. 4: Stand Out for the Right Reasons**

- Don't be Your Assistant or the Lunch Girl — 68
- Organizing Non-Work Matters — 69
- Pick Your Battles—Sharing a Controversial Opinion — 70
- Knowledge is Power in Negotiations — 71
- Being a Whistleblower — 72
- Monitor Your Emotions — 73
- Avoid Being Too Easily Offended—Difficult Personalities — 73
- Male Banter—The Boys' Club — 74

— Be Confident, Not Difficult	74
— Be Statuesque rather than Sexy	76
— Don't Date a Colleague or Superior	78
— You Don't Have to Be a Sports Fan to Be Interesting	80
— You Don't Have to Work All Night to be respected	81
— Don't Be That Girl—Slut or Drunk	81

Chapter 5
Building Relationships for Long Term Success 83

> Rule No. 5: Strategize and Build Positive Relationships

— Get to Know Your Team Leaders and Management	83
— Be a Team Player; Build Relationships	83
— Learn from Role Models	84
— Seek Suitable Mentors—Inside or Outside of the Office	84
— Find a Sponsor or Advocate within Your Company	87
— Recruit Allies: How Men Can Help	88
— Breaking Into the 'Boys' Club':	88
➤ Meaning of the Boys' Club	88
➤ The Dilemma of Tolerating Bad Behavior	89
➤ Using the 'Boys Club' to Your Advantage	89
➤ How to Break into the Boys' Club	92
— Create Your Own Girls' Club or Women's Mentoring Network	93
➤ Create Your Board of Directors Outside of Work	94
➤ Building a Network of Women Outside of the Office	95

Chapter 6
The Importance of Marketing Skills 96

> Rule No. 6: Use Available Resources

— The Importance of Learning Marketing Skills	96
— Build-Out Your Network of Contacts	97
— Develop Your Elevator Speech and Brand	98

— Get to Know and Appreciate Your Clients, Customers, and Vendors, and Add to Your Network of Contacts	99
— Identify New Targets for Marketing Purposes—Once a Week	100
— Working Your Target	101
— Developing a Personal Relationship with Your Client Is Key	103
— Avoid Being a "Know it All;" Instead, Foster Trust	104
— Ask for Introductions and Referrals	105
— Using Social Media (The Do's and Don'ts)	105
— Protect Your Turf	106

Chapter 7
Find Your Voice and Toot Your Horn; Be Visible — 109

> **Rule No. 7: Be Heard Loud and Clear**

— Speak Up for Yourself; Be Assertive	109
— Make Yourself Known during Meetings	110
— Showcase Your Abilities and Successes	111
— How to Impress When You Are Working Remotely	111
— Mastering Self-Promotion	114
— Use Past Accomplishments to Your Advantage	114
— Highlight Positive Actions You Have Taken	114
— Go the Extra Mile	116
— Managing Workloads; Setting Work Boundaries	116
— If You See a Teaching Moment, Take Advantage!	117
— Don't Tolerate Interruptions, Stealing of Ideas, or Disrespectful Behavior:	119
› Meetings with Colleagues	119
› Meetings with Clients or Customers	121
› Remind Colleagues Not to Be a Bystander	123
› Support Your Female Colleagues	123
— Conquering the Dreaded Performance Review	124
› Preparing for Your Performance Review	125
— Negotiating Your Salary	127
› Do Your Research	128

- ➤ Avoid Stating Your Current Salary — 130
- ➤ Create a Satisfactory Range — 130
- ➤ Set Expectations Early — 131
- ➤ Don't Settle for Low — 131
- Negotiating for a Raise or Promotion in Your Existing Job — 132
  - ➤ How to Ask for a Raise or Promotion — 133

Chapter 8
Maintaining Balance at Work and Relieving Stress — 136

> ➤ **Rule No. 8: Prioritize Safe and Healthy Play**

- Hundreds Have Preceded You—You Can Do It — 136
- The "30 Minute Rule" — 137
- Ask for Help — 137
- Take Breaks for Your Health and Career — 138
- Organize Your Home Life (Like You Do Your Job) — 139
- Prioritize Mind & Body; Take Care of Yourself — 141
- Maternity Leave/Mommy Track/Adjusting Your Schedule — 142
- Take Advantage of Company Benefits (Mental Health, Childcare, etc.) — 149

Chapter 9
Fostering Respect in The Workplace — 152

> ➤ **Rule No. 9: Command Respect from the Players on the Playground**

- The Golden Rule Regarding How to Treat Others — 152
- The Impact of the COVID-19 Pandemic on Working Women: — 153
  - ➤ The Clock Has Turned Back on Gender Equality and Discrimination — 153
  - ➤ Protect Yourself from Objectionable Behavior by Colleagues or Executives — 157
  - ➤ Remind Your Employer about the Importance of Supporting Working Mothers — 158

- ➤ How Can Employers Help? 159
- Is There a Silver Lining for Working Remotely? 160
- Women Supporting Women 161
- Toxic Work Environment 166
  - ➤ My Personal Experiences Practicing Law 169
  - ➤ Dealing with Bullies 172
  - ➤ Dealing with a Narcissist 175
  - ➤ How do you deal with a narcissist? 176
  - ➤ Dealing with a Chauvinist 177
  - ➤ How should you deal with a chauvinist? 179
  - ➤ Dealing with Sexual Harassment—Pick Your Battles 180
  - ➤ Draw a Hard Line of Respect 180
  - ➤ Don't Be One of the Boys 182
  - ➤ What if Your Customer or Client is the Harasser, Male or Female? 183
  - ➤ *Play Nice*—Playground Rules for Respect in the Workplace 184
  - ➤ Share Your Opinion—Gently 185
- Identify and Use Your Allies 186
- Being the Manager or Supervisor 187

Chapter 10
How Men Can Help Their Female Colleagues 189

> ➤ **Rule No. 10: Support Your Fellow Players**

- Use Every Opportunity to Educate Your Male Counterparts About the Value Women Bring to the Table to Encourage Their Support: 189
- Why Women Are Good Leaders 194
- Unconscious Bias, Gender Discrimination, and Sexual Harassment 196
- Don't be a Bystander 197
  - ➤ What About in the Business World? 198
- Ask Your Male Colleague to Become an Advocate 201
- Support Female-Friendly Policies for Promotion and Hiring into Leadership Roles 201

Chapter 11
How Your Company Can Help Break the Glass Ceiling   202

> Rule No. 11: Promote Equality, Fairness and Safety

— Promoting Workplace Cultural Change   202
— Goals for Consideration to Help Effect Change: 202
  - Transparency in Policies and Enforcement   202
  - 'Zero Tolerance' Directives   203
  - Anonymous Complaint System   203
  - Unconscious Bias Training   203
  - Establish Mentoring and Educational Programs   203
  - Develop More Female Leadership   204
  - Foster Diversity Hiring and Promotion   204
  - Provide Equal Opportunities for Work and Promotion   204
  - Establish Female Friendly Recruiting Practices   204
  - Audit Hiring and Promotion Practices for Transparency and Equality   205
  - Audit Compensation for Transparency and Equality   205
  - Create Flexible Work Environments   205
  - Provide Generous Paid Parental Leave and Substantive Reintegration upon Return   206
  - Provide Affordable and Accessible Childcare   206

Conclusion   209
Acknowledgements   213
Notes   215
About the Author   235

Authors' Note

HAS ANYTHING CHANGED?

It was on a holiday weekend years ago when I was still practicing law. I took advantage of the quiet office and spent a day cleaning my desk and getting my files organized for the upcoming week. Instead of my usual medley of soft rock music, I turned the TV on for entertainment. My interest peaked when I realized the show I was watching was highlighting instances of gender discrimination—*Sirens*, a sitcom involving three male EMTs (one of whom is gay). In the episode of interest, all three EMTs end up at a wedding for a gay couple. During the wedding reception, the gay EMT proudly introduces his friend, a policewoman, "as one of the best cops in Chicago" to his other policeman friend to set them up romantically and walks off to get drinks for the group. When he returns, he hears his male friend taunting his female counterpart: "Women are not meant to be on the force. You cannot handle extreme situations and are a liability!" As his insults escalate, the policewoman tries to remain calm. "What's wrong?" he continues. You can't handle my comments? What are you going to do? Kick me in the nuts?"

Eventually, the scene ends with the gay EMT consoling the offending policeman with a bag of ice and the following advice: "Dude— you need to either stop underestimating women or wear a cup!"

Sure, this scene was part of a new comedy series intending to invoke laughter and entertainment; however, the writers of *Sirens* made a point of using this episode to illustrate a typical gender discrimination scenario to educate their male audience on their pivotal role in helping to eliminate sexual harassment and discrimination against women generally. As a viewer all too familiar with gender biases in the workplace, it was good to see a popular show use its platform to confront the issue of sex-based discrimination and offer an effective way to address it.

Later, I came across an old *Law and Order* episode which first aired on May 5, 1998, more than 25 years ago. Progressive for its time. Incidentally, the very first scene I watched contained an encounter involving workplace-gender dynamics. The scene depicted the female, Lt. Van Buren, talking to a male Detective, Curtis, about his request for desk duty after he was nearly killed in a shooting. Van Buren stopped Curtis in the hall and told him, "I got your request, but now is not a good time." He replies: "My request is serious!" She responds: "I appreciate your wife's desire to see you at a desk job, but I can't afford to lose a detective right now. If I lose you, my bosses won't replace you with a new detective." Curtis' next response surprised me. "Chief, my family has to come first." Van Buren ignored his concern and walked away.

This edgy scene contrasts gender workplace norms at the time this show aired. Foremost, a female superior and male subordinate contradicts the then-prevailing gender stereotypes, which continuously depicted males as inherently dominant. Even more compelling are the instances of non-stereotypical gender behavior portrayed by either employee. Curtis' desire to appease his wife's concerns reveals an unexpected male display of affection. At the same time, Van Buren's negligence of Curtis' feelings depicts her as a demanding female superior. The writers challenge traditional gender roles and stereotypes to promote gender equality. They use their platform to demonstrate how women can also hold positions of power and dominance and that men can also exhibit sensitivity and emotional vulnerability without affecting their masculinity. This portrayal, catalyzed by the show's platform, helps to break down gender barriers, encouraging viewers to be more open-minded and accepting of diverse representations of gender.

As I continued to watch other shows over the weekend, I noted many gender-related undertones. Surely, these messages were intentional, and they beg the question: What are we meant to learn from these depictions, which either reinforce or contradict gender stereotypes in the workplace?

Let's fast forward to more current shows like *Castle*, which first aired on March 9, 2009. *Castle's* main character, Beckett, is a female detective. Her superior, female Captain Victoria Gates, is no-nonsense and has a very tough personality, so tough that she insists on being addressed as "Sir." Why, you may ask? Well, at first, this seems odd.

When considering Captain Gate's perspective, her taxing job consists of commanding a fleet of mostly male detectives and police officers while simultaneously juggling her male superiors' demands and politics—and managing Beckett, a strong-willed and determined female cop. Given the challenges of her job and hefty workload, Gates did not want to be seen as weak or risk being second-guessed or disrespected. But does her insistence on being addressed as "Sir" make her appear less than herself? What message does this send to women in the workforce? Is her title, earned after many years of hard work, insufficient to command the respect she deserves? Does she have to embody a more masculine persona to be taken seriously?

Let's consider *Rizzoli & Isles*, another popular crime series first aired in July of 2010, starring Angie Harmon as Rizzoli and Sasha Alexander as Isles. Rizzoli, a Boston detective, is an attractive single woman who prefers to wear pants and conservative colors on and off duty. By contrast, Isles, the chief medical examiner and Rizzoli's best bud on the show, wears beautiful shapely skirts, dresses, and high heels—even at crime scenes (which Rizzoli does not hesitate to mock).

Isles appears very feminine, while Rizzoli does not. This contrast in appearances was undoubtedly intended to showcase their personalities. Rizzoli plays a tough female cop who despises weak behavior and emotion—socially deemed unacceptable for women detectives like herself. How did her young female viewers perceive Rizzoli's attitude and behavior? Is she viewed as suppressing feelings and emotions to help her survive in a male-dominated environment? What about Isles? She is the chief medical examiner—a beautiful woman who readily shows emotion. Does her earned title as a doctor allow her to be truer to herself and less likely to be challenged? Or is it simply that she is more confident in her role and as a female in her male-dominated environment (as opposed to Rizzoli)?

After taking note of these various examples, I had many questions. What underlying messages do these shows aim to convey? Let's delve into the characters of Van Buren in *Law and Order*, Beckett in *Castle*, and Rizzoli in *Rizzoli & Isles*. Is it a prerequisite for women to embody traits such as physical toughness, harshness, aloofness, and emotional detachment to thrive in male-dominated professions? Must they conform to masculine standards in behavior and appearance to garner respect for their accomplishments? I don't think this is true, although throughout my years, including today, I have encountered many women who would strongly disagree with my opinion. They believe that true success necessitates being tough as nails and taking on male traits, including being non-empathetic and harsh.

These days, we hear that women should not "act like our male counterparts" or "dress like a man." Doing so makes us unattractive. Yet, it is reality that women must work long, often unreasonable hours, surpass expectations, outwork their male counterparts, and navigate through gender discrimination, pay disparities, and harassment for advancement. Although ideally, it is important for us women to remain "true to ourselves and how we are as a person" and to "make our own mark as we progress through the ranks," this comes at a great cost.

For many, suppressing your true self to fight for more senior positions is not worth the sacrifice. Eventually, these women leave their companies exhausted, resorting to less challenging jobs with fewer hours and less pay. This remains true today. Sadly, the landscape seems unchanged since my departure from the workforce nine years ago.

I firmly believe you can learn how to set boundaries and demand the respect required without coming across as being "bitchy" or "difficult."

It is possible to assert yourself successfully without compromising your authenticity. However, you must learn how to speak up for yourself and develop the skills necessary to navigate common challenges faced by women in male-dominated environments.

Play Smart, the second book of The Sandbox Series, is a comprehensive guide packed with insightful research, personal anecdotes, and practical strategies designed to empower women in male-dominated environments. Additionally, it aims to educate men on the challenges women encounter in the workplace and how to become better allies.

Please note that although many of my personal anecdotes and research relate to my past practice as an attorney, the concepts apply to any field of work and are worthy of consideration regardless of where you may be in your career.

Within the pages of this book, you will discover techniques to overcome barriers and achieve professional excellence, cultivate a professional network, advocate for yourself, set boundaries with colleagues, address gender bias, negotiate fair compensation, seek proper sponsors and mentorship, balance parenthood with career aspirations, and deal effectively with the boys' club—all with poise and confidence.

Don't let gender bias or unequal pay hold you back. *Play Smart* and arm yourself with the crucial skills you need to shatter the glass ceiling for success and create a more fulfilling and prosperous career path!

Introduction

The False Perception of Equal Opportunity

I recently talked with a senior law partner friend who insisted women no longer face gender-based workplace issues. He claimed that the pendulum now swung against men. One example he used to support this claim was that women at his company were organizing coveted "best practices" marketing and client development meetings to exclude men, thus giving women a "critical" advantage in bringing new clients and businesses to his law firm. "Unacceptable," he said. "If men are not allowed to have 'men-only meetings' anymore, then women should not be permitted to do so either." None of my arguments changed his mind. I tried.

It did not matter that, for decades, women (whether in companies or law firms) were excluded from similar meetings involving strategizing about important transactions and marketing opportunities. It did not matter that, for decades, women had been stripped of countless opportunities to participate in business development activities, including bonding events tailored to "men only" (lavish dinners, golfing, hunting, fishing, cigar bars, and, yes, strip clubs). DECADES.

It also did not matter men statistically hand business opportunities to men over women due to engrained gender discrimination and implicit biases. "One in ten working women say they have been passed over for the most important assignments because of their gender, compared with 5% of men."[1]

Furthermore, there are proven facts that women and minorities bear the brunt of bad behavior in the workplace (regardless of industry), including discrimination, implicit bias, bullying, and sexual harassment. [Id.]

My lawyer friend was unimpressed despite my recounting of instances of workplace discrimination against women and minorities based on gender. These instances included women receiving less pay than men despite having similar job responsibilities, women being evaluated to be less competent due to gender, women receiving less support from senior leadership, women being passed over for promotions or slighted for important opportunities due to gender or pregnancy, and women being subjected to unwanted advances.[2] My senior law partner friend didn't think that statistics would help me drive in my points. So, I set out to educate him using credible statistics.

The research I carried out suggested that "About four in ten working women (42%) in the United States say they have faced discrimination on the job because of their gender."[3] In the legal industry for example, only 38% of attorneys at law firms are women, 27% of all partners are women, and women hold only 30% of U.S. law firms' executive or management committee positions.[4]

Women of color remain highly underrepresented and continue to face challenges concerning proper mentorship, opportunities for progression, and equal pay. Despite making up 20% of first-year law students, women of color represent only 9% of attorneys, 4% of all partners, and about 3% of equity partners at law firms. Id. These statistics are simply unacceptable and prove that the pendulum has yet to swing fully in favor of women. There is much more work to do. You would think law firms especially would have a heightened sensitivity to providing equal opportunities for women and minorities and strict zero tolerance policies against discrimination.

Unfortunately, women are leaving law firms in greater numbers because of gender discrimination—impacting pay inequities, work assignments, and opportunities for promotion.[5] The COVID-19 pandemic further complicated the experience for working mothers, making it challenging to balance a busy work schedule with caregiving responsibilities. We'll discuss this subject more in a later chapter. *[The COVID-19 pandemic, also known as the coronavirus pandemic, is a global outbreak of the novel SARS-CoV-2, first identified in Wuhan, China, in December 2019 and declared a pandemic on March 11, 2020.]*

In the United States, gender discrimination violates the law under Title VII of the Civil Rights Act of 1964. This federal law prohibits employment discrimination based on race, color, religion, gender, or national origin. Despite the illegality, gender bias in the workplace continues even today, negatively affecting women, women of color, and transgender women.[6]

It is unfortunate that anti-discrimination laws do not always protect against discriminatory practices. Only a few states in the U.S. require or even recommend that companies implement anti-harassment policies.[7]

The EEOC Task Force Report recommends that "Companies adopt a robust anti-harassment policy, regularly train each employee on its contents, and vigorously follow and enforce the policy." However, it is important to note that in certain states (such as Tennessee), if a company adopts an anti-harassment policy, the employer may use it as a defense against an employee's sexual harassment claim. This means that if the employee has not timely followed all applicable company policy requirements when filing the complaint, the claim fails, and the company is protected at the expense of the employee.[8]

Although more companies implemented anti-sexual harassment and discrimination policies in response to the explosion of the #MeToo movement in 2017,[9] I believe *many* companies only did so for the sake of "appearances" and not with genuine intent to protect its employees with zero tolerance.

If senior management does not believe that anti-sexual harassment and discrimination policies are needed to protect its employees, who then will set the tone for gender discrimination and sexual harassment to be taken seriously? It only takes one bad apple to trigger millions in monetary loss to a company in value of stock and/or lawsuit damages. For more on this subject, check out the first book of The Sandbox Series, *Play Nice—Playground Rules for Respect in the Workplace*, which focuses on how to deal with sexual harassment and other bad behavior in and outside of the workplace.[10]

A research paper from the AllVoices Team from September 1, 2021, surveyed 832 employees to gain insights on sexual harassment, workplace harassment, and discrimination; they found out that:

- ✓ 44% have experienced harassment at work.
- ✓ 38% still experienced harassment working remotely, through email, video conferencing, chat apps, or phone conversations.
- ✓ 34% have left their jobs because of unresolved harassment issues.
- ✓ 26% have remained in the workplace despite *ongoing* issues of harassment.
- ✓ 85% are more likely to report harassment if they have an anonymous channel.
- ✓ Only 72% believe their workplace wants harassment reported.
- ✓ 28% say their workplace does not encourage employees to raise harassment issues.[11]

Other research from 2015 to 2020 indicates that more than 63% of 2,400 female candidates interviewed said they felt discriminated against in the workplace due to their gender, compared to just 7% of men.[12] Statistics show that 50% of women primarily felt gender discrimination in unequal pay, 30% experienced bias during interviews, 26% experienced sexual harassment, and 76% were not taken seriously. Id.

The statistics speak for themselves. Yet, when I shared these compelling facts with my senior law partner friend, he still did not believe me. He triumphantly directed me to a successful female colleague in his office who he described as a "warrior." She was strong, intelligent, reliable, and capable of handling complex tasks. In his mind, her attitude proved that she endured no gender discrimination. After I questioned him further, he admitted that there had been times when a client insisted on hiring a man. This request compelled him to direct the work to one of her male colleagues. "However," he said, "this female colleague is successful and proof that the statistics could not be correct."

Describing her as a "warrior" tells us that she was tough and capable of dealing with and enduring discrimination. However, despite her standing, she still suffered gender discrimination when the client insisted on a male attorney and the senior law partner did not try to convince the client of her capabilities.

What about other female colleagues who are not warriors? I asked. Were they viewed equally as capable and respected compared to their male colleagues? Are all of them treated fairly, without gender discrimination? After all, statistics are about numbers.

Only 25% of the attorneys at his firm are women, well below the approximate 38% national average. More women would mean more voices to influence the firm's status quo and level the playing field for equality between men and women. This is true for any work industry.

In response to my male attorney friend's complaint about "women-only meetings," these spaces actually address the workplace disadvantages of unequal rights and opportunities women and minorities continue to face. If women in a company decide to create women-only meetings or other events to help improve their marketing skills, which are needed to *catch up with men* and *help women succeed in their work environment*, their efforts should be supported and applauded.

As we will discuss further later in this book, these efforts will likely foster a healthier work environment, benefiting the employer financially. Women-only meetings or other events should only be viewed as discriminatory against men once equal parity is reached regarding treatment and opportunities for women.

In many cases, the female-only meetings are designed to provide a "safe space" for sensitive discussions on topics that might be hard for women to discuss in the presence of men. In other cases, as noted, they are designed to help women "catch up" and achieve equal opportunities as men. As Dr. Rashmee advises, "The basis of [substantive equality] is that there's an acknowledgment that everyone in society is not born with equal opportunities to succeed. Society isn't on a level playing field.

As such, we must treat certain groups differently to ensure those left behind have extra support." [13]

Essentially, women do not form "women-only clubs from a position of achieving power or to overrule their male colleagues or counterparts. Singh sees "women clubs as a way to bring the women up to where the men are". [Id.] Thus, they are bridging gender gaps within the work environment.

Five years ago, the Dallas Bar Association launched WE LEAD, a dynamic platform of empowerment and education for 25 to 30 highly qualified women each year to combat the evident reality of gender disparity in the legal industry concerning pay, work opportunities, advancement, and visibility. WE LEAD was launched after the Texas Women's Foundation concluded that "high-performing women attorneys with 8 to 15 years of practice are all too often constrained and undermined by the entrenched biases and conventions of a profession historically dominated by men."[14] Harriet Miers noted in 2018: "This innovative program will help women lawyers by increasing their opportunities for leadership and financial success in the profession, but also help ensure our profession models the balance and fairness it should." Among her many high-profile accomplishments, Harriet Miers served as White House Counsel to George W. Bush from 2005 to 2007. Hopefully, other legal and non-legal associations will follow suit and develop similar programs.

It is important to help men understand the daily biases women face in the work environment. Despite the risk of uncomfortable discussions, I recommend that men be included in specific conversations to endear them to the plight of women and minorities, helping them understand and thus be more supportive of the female work experience. Witnessing sensitive discussions and hearing personal accounts is critical to educating men, from top management to junior male colleagues, since inappropriate behavior and unconscious bias occur at all levels and in all work environments. By including men in sensitive discussions, we can foster better solutions and achieve greater gender equality.

Additionally, suppose meetings include best business development practices. In that case, it might be valuable for women to learn what tools work in the business world from male mentors, especially when dealing with other men. Our male colleagues are important as allies, advocates, and mentors to help with client introductions and opportunities for advancement. Regardless of discussion topics, both sides will undoubtedly learn from open and informative dialogue.

Finally, I must address my male attorney friend's belief that "men are not permitted to have 'male events' anymore." This claim is simply inaccurate. The 'boys' club' continues to be alive and well, and plenty of male-bonding events occur where female participation is neither encouraged nor welcome. I will share more later on the boys' club and the importance of male mentorship.

Regardless of whether your company supports women-only meetings and events, women must be proactive about helping themselves to bond and educate. Such efforts should be encouraged, applauded, and rewarded, especially by senior female and male colleagues.

We Have Not Come Far Enough

I was at lunch with my husband's old work friends a few years ago. One of them brought his daughter, a college senior at the time. We were in deep discussions about the job market and where she might want to work, when one of the guys offered her an interview at his company, a prominent real estate firm. The opportunity was square within her interests.

Her father leaned over to her and said, "This Company is very male-dominated. If you were the lucky candidate to get that job, you would have to be prepared to deal with gender discrimination and sexual harassment, and lots of male banter and sexual innuendos."

I turned to the potential employer and asked whether the company had policies against sexual harassment and gender discrimination. He responded as expected for a company of his size: "Of course we do." Then came the lengthy discussion among the group at lunch about the reality of company policy enforcement and the importance of learning how to stop bad behavior when it occurs without having to first complain to the company's Human Resources department (which we will call ("HR")). All agreed that as a woman, working in this male-dominated environment would not be without its challenges. This lunch group included the same men who accompanied my journey in writing *Play Nice* as a sounding board—open to education on the plight of women concerning sexual harassment and discrimination. Their male perspectives were treasured.

In a perfect world, you would enter a work environment where gender equality concerning salaries, opportunity, and promotion is prioritized, policies and procedures against bullying, discrimination, and sexual harassment are progressive, and violations are enforced on a zero-tolerance basis. There would also be regular education for executives and staff on the importance of fair and equal treatment in the workplace.

Unfortunately, even if some companies claim to have protective policies, they provide no guarantee that you will be treated fairly; most times, they only serve as mere window dressing. I also observed that many companies lack equipped HR departments to properly assist with violations, complaints, or enforcement. Sadly, many companies are deficient in programs necessary to train their executives and employees regarding discrimination, bullying, sexual harassment, and proper leadership skills.

As a woman, the likelihood of being treated fairly is not high if you work in a male-dominated environment.

Here are a few more statistics: Roughly 60% of managers are men, as opposed to 40% women. This gender disparity widens as you climb the corporate ladder. In the C-suite (where you will find the highest-ranking senior executives in an organization—the letter "C" represents the word "chief" in many corporate titles), only one in four executives are women. At the same time, less than one in 25 are women of color.[15]

According to recent studies, women in the United States are paid 20% less than men on average. This pay gap stretches further for minorities and women of color. Black women are paid 38% less, and Latinas are paid 47% less than men. The pay gap extends even more among higher-paying industries and roles.[16]

Not much has changed according to the statistics. Gender discrimination continues to prevail.

The Goal of *Play Smart*

My co-author for the first book *Play Nice*, JR, and I met in 2002 at a women's networking luncheon. At the time, I was a commercial real estate and finance law partner at a mid-sized law firm in Dallas, Texas. At the same time, JR was a commercial real-estate broker at a local company in Dallas. Both of our industries were, and still are, heavily male-dominated. Throughout the many years we have known each other, JR and I have raged over appalling workplace experiences of sexual harassment, abuse, blatant gender discrimination, and the troubling frequency of such occurrences. What we both discovered through our discussions with colleagues, other professionals, friends, and family, including many younger members of our respective fields, are saddening realities. Despite over thirty years since JR and I started our respective careers, there has only been a slight improvement in the toxic masculinity of workplace culture and in company policies intended to combat gender discrimination, implicit bias, bullying, and sexual harassment. Worse, news stories have repeatedly confirmed that filing a complaint with the HR department—assuming you have access to an HR department—will not necessarily save your job. The potential for retaliation, humiliation, bullying, and even termination remain genuine risks that can be dire and destructive.

What is striking is even in today's environment where disclosure of bad behavior is encouraged, we have found that young women who recently entered the workforce are afraid to publicly share their gender discrimination and sexual harassment experiences out of fears of retaliation and loss of job promotion opportunities—even if their names and employers remain unidentified. Under what circumstances would this saddening trend ever be acceptable? It is heartbreaking.

JR and I agreed that one day, we would publish our collective advice on handling a male-dominated work environment by sharing the strategies we believe helped us succeed. When we finally began our book journey for *Play Nice* in the summer of 2017, the #MeToo movement exploded. What we thought would be one single chapter about sexual harassment in the workplace quickly became an entire book—a comprehensive guide and educational tool for victims and bystanders seeking advice on how to deal with an abuser on the spot. Additionally, *Play Nice* is an important resource for HR professionals and company leaders to improve their company's policies and procedures, helping them promote a work culture free of discrimination, bullying, and sexual harassment. *Play Nice—Playground Rules for Respect in the Workplace*, was published in 2019. For our book and my blogs and lessons on the subjects covered by *Play Nice*, please see our website.[17]

Surprisingly, the launch of #MeToo in the fall of 2017 and the continued outing of violators, resulting in severe consequences to careers, reputations, and company profitability, has not deterred lousy behavior. Today, almost seven years later, sexual harassment persists, and headlines cover new violators regularly. Our book *Play Nice* continues to be relevant for anyone who wants to enter or is already in the workforce, whether victim, bystander, or employer.[18]

Companies' attempts to implement proper policies and procedures and the subsequent legal changes designed to protect those violated have not fostered sufficient progress. Women continue to face challenges in the workplace, including gender discrimination regarding salaries, opportunities, and promotion, persistent bullying, and yes, you guessed it—sexual harassment. Making matters worse, the COVID-19 pandemic reversed much of the progress made eradicating these challenges for working women, a topic discussed later in this book.

I decided it was time to implement our original intention for our first book, *Play Smart—Playground Strategies for Success in a Male-Dominated Workplace*, a comprehensive guide on how to break through the "glass ceiling" with grace and confidence without giving anyone a reason to challenge your abilities on achieving your career goals. In this book, I will share my work experiences which gave me more to talk about than I could have ever imagined on how to *Play Smart* at work!

The Meaning of the Sandbox on the Playground of the Work Environment

As I described in the first book, *Play Nice*, it takes time to create a positive culture in a thriving workplace or business that fosters morale, loyalty, and dedication. Organizations must put consistent efforts into their work environment to ensure cultural longevity, allowing them to remain strong over time. Workplace culture is an essential part of the working environment—the "playground" of a business. The term "playground" is used to highlight simple behavioral rules we all learned as children to reframe [emphasize] the message of each chapter of this book for more effective communication.

The sandbox in this playground is where we imagine men and women working, collaborating, receiving mentorship, developing ideas, completing projects, and where the success of any business is ultimately measured. The sandbox is a crucial component of any business and, thus, should be a positive and healthy environment populated by both men and women. These individuals should have a complement of strengths and weaknesses and a diverse culture for age, gender identity, biological sex, sexual orientation, race, ethnicity, and disability. The sandbox should have leadership that commands mutual respect, healthy mentorship, and an environment free of bigotry, gender bias, bullying, and sexual harassment. Once the sandbox does not succeed in any of these areas, the health and success of businesses will likely suffer adverse consequences that will further negatively impact profitability. For example, since the launch of the #MeToo movement, there have been dozens of examples of high-dollar lawsuit settlements, ruined careers, and expensive company failures, involving Fox News, CNN, CBS, Wallstreet, the NFL, and many others, all based on the failure of their "sandboxes."

It is in every company's best interest to foster a work environment free of gender discrimination that pertains to salary, opportunity, promotion, bigotry, racism, and sexual harassment.

Being Proactive is Key

Achieving parity with male counterparts regarding equal pay, treatment, and opportunity will likely take many more years. We need more effective legislation with noteworthy consequences to deter violations in combating sexist, male-dominated work culture and the accompanying bad behavior. Additionally, we need many more women in executive-level positions in the workforce.

Introduction

Until then, my counsel is that women should take control of their careers by navigating obstacles with common sense and seeking help from role models and mentors, regardless of gender. Don't wait for others to pave the way; instead, forge your own path to success.

1

Understanding The Obstacles and Potential Barriers to Career Progression

Evaluate and Understand the Risks before you enter the Playground, this is vital.

The playground is your work environment. So, before you step into a new work environment's sandbox, ensure you do your research on the company's policies and reputation. Include all information on senior executives in your research to help determine how these executives might treat you as an employee. You want to enter your job with a better understanding of any risks so you can prepare yourself to address them appropriately if needed.

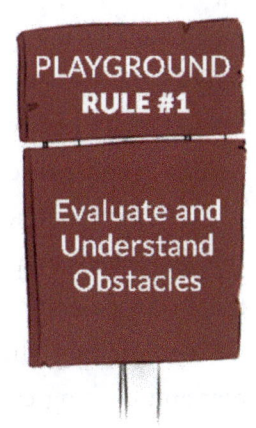

PLAYGROUND RULE #1

Evaluate and Understand Obstacles

Search online for any message boards, lawsuits, news stories, or ex-employee reviews (for example, Glassdoor) to get a sense of the company culture before you apply or accept an offer from them. Talk to former or current employees willing to share their experiences dealing with senior executives who might prove difficult and any work environment cultural issues they may find challenging. Here are some questions: Is there diversity of thought and perspective within the organization? Will you be able to speak freely and share your thoughts and opinions? Does the company hire a variety of applicants at all levels? Do you think management and coworkers will look out for you? Is having a family encouraged? Is there a progressive maternity leave policy? How are new mothers treated when they return from their maternity leave?

Review the parameters of your job position with your future superiors to confirm if there is a mutual understanding regarding the nature and scope of your work responsibilities. This is essential so that you do not continuously end up tasked with work that is either above your pay grade (without proper compensation) or that other staff should handle.

Determine how your department is structured. Will you have one or more supervisors to provide guidance and proper training when needed? Does the company have up to date policies and procedures to prevent sexual harassment, bullying, and discrimination led by a capable HR department? Are they supported by senior management who enforce these policies firmly? Google about the company and its senior executives to find out if there have been any recent problems or lawsuits. Use keywords like sexual harassment, employment discrimination, gender discrimination, pay equality, lawsuit, settlement, etc.

Inquire about advancement opportunities for women and minorities. Does the company have a positive track record and reputation? Is there transparency regarding pay, opportunities, and promotion?

Researching these issues online and communicating with former and existing employees is an effective tool for gathering valuable information.

As we have noted, there is no guarantee you will be treated fairly as a working woman. Only some companies tick all the boxes to these questions in a positive manner. Conducting all this research will help you prepare how to handle any obstacles, negative situations, or barriers you might face to thrive in your career. Additionally, you can ask for more practical help to address them.

Meeting your future superiors to discuss your role and potential for promotion may also help. In today's climate post COVID-19 pandemic, there are more opportunities for follow-up video conferencing calls if personal meetings are not convenient.

However, be warned. There is never a guarantee that you will get all of your questions answered or that the responses you get will accurately reflect the company's actual working culture.

If you are not comfortable asking senior management these questions, ask to meet your future colleagues in a more casual setting to address your concerns and get a feel for their comments about their work, superiors, and career progression. Meet with former employees to find out what they liked or did not like about their job. Ask them why they left the company. Were any of them worried about a toxic work environment? You need to know. I'll discuss more on this later.

Once you accept a position, don't stop asking questions. You will have to be proactive. Understand the obstacles you may face as you mature through the ranks, learn the tools necessary to combat discrimination or other inappropriate behavior and inform your teams and superiors of what you need to progress and succeed, especially in a male-dominated environment. Unconscious bias, gender inequities, and discrimination continue to be alive and well in and outside of the workplace. You must be proactive to stop bad behavior even before it begins.

As I have noted, not much has changed since I entered the workforce thirty-plus years ago.

Breaking The Glass Ceiling—It is Not a Myth

Imagine starting a new job you worked hard to earn. You get up early, dress your best, and show up believing your new employer's promises of gender equality are true: you will be treated fairly with equal pay, opportunities, and promotion. You will not have to face a "Glass Ceiling," or will you?

At a recent gathering, a male friend of mine triumphantly declared that the glass ceiling did not exist anymore—especially not after the explosion of #MeToo in late 2017. "This movement shamed companies into changing their ways and implementing equality in hiring, opportunity, and salary," adding, "and now they are hiring unqualified candidates to the detriment of men." As he finished his sentence, he could see my facial expression had changed.

I wasn't surprised by his declaration, just disappointed that he wasn't enlightened about the statistics and trends identified throughout all the turmoil of the last seven years, including high profile news stories outing shameful behavior and company failures, the many demonstrations for Women's Rights and Black Lives Matter, and the negative impact of the COVID-19 pandemic on women in the workforce. My friend is a senior executive at his company. He is in a position of influence with several daughters about to graduate from college. From prior discussions, I knew he was concerned about what his daughters would face in the job market, so I got to work on educating him.

First, we discussed the meaning of "Glass Ceiling." The term is a metaphor for an invisible barrier that prevents specific demographic groups (often women and other minorities) from moving into senior positions, whether through promotions, pay raises, or opportunities for higher-profile projects and activities, despite their qualifications and achievements. The "Glass Ceiling" is a subtle but damaging form of discrimination.[1]

Research confirms that "the glass ceiling still exists across various industries for different groups of people. Men still occupy most executive positions in corporations and other positions of power. Although the barriers get more attention, they are still very much present in the workforce."[2]

According to statistics, "In 2021, women accounted for 56.8% of the labor force in the U.S., but when it came to chief executive positions, women held only 29.1% of these roles, and 85.7% of chief executives identified as white, according to the Bureau of Labor Statistics (BLS)." Id. According to the 2021 "Women CEOs in America" report, "there were 41 female CEOs of Fortune 500 companies," only "five of which are women of color." [3]

For black women, LGBTQ+ women, and women of color, barriers to leadership positions are more prominent. Further, these women are more likely to experience offensive and insensitive statements or questions (micro-aggressions) related to gender, sexual identity, ethnicity, and race.[4]

Making matters worse, women are often the default parent for childcare or aging parents, requiring more flexible work arrangements which in turn "make [women] less visible to people who are making decisions about who is a star performer or who should get promotions," according to Rosalind M. Chow.[5]

The U.S. Department of Labor's Glass Ceiling Commission discovered that "qualified women and minorities got several denied opportunities to compete for or win decision-making positions." [6] Allowing the glass ceiling in a work environment perpetuates a form of discrimination that prevents women from working in positions commensurate with their level of competence. The existence of the "Glass Ceiling" is supported by research discovering that women are 18 percent less likely to be promoted than their male counterparts.[7]

Sexism still looms large, and the persistence of sexist attitudes and beliefs only serves to reinforce the Glass Ceiling. This insidious barrier inhibits women's progress.

For example, it is a widely held belief that women are more emotional and not as tough as their male counterparts. They do not have what it takes for leadership and progression, especially if they have entered motherhood. Moreover, it is generally believed that women are better suited in their biological roles of mother and spouse, deeming them less committed and unable to work long hours compared to their male counterparts, especially in leadership positions.[8]

By contrast, many believe men to be more competent, intelligent, and physically stronger than women, thus better suited to occupy several management and leadership positions.

It is further believed that for a woman to be successful, she must be ruthless, competitive, and cold. Interesting, since women who are perceived as such are not generally liked or found attractive. We hear statements like, "Women should not act like men nor take on traits that are reserved for men, as that makes them less attractive." However, if a woman is attractive, male superiors might deem her a "distraction" and decide not to offer her any advancement opportunities.

Recently, a potential new hire was informed by a superior that she would not be permitted to travel with male colleagues since their wives might complain and to avoid male temptation. It was implied that her good looks made her a "temptress." She was forced to make an unacceptable career decision. If she took the job, she would be excluded and discriminated against for her sleek and gorgeous looks, likely missing out on important work opportunities—such exclusion potentially harmful to her career. She could have complained to HR about the superior's interview statements; however, complaining might have been risky and might have drawn negative consequences for her, not the superior. This scenario occurred at a high-profile company, and it's another example of gender discrimination at its best.

Today, despite the issues and concerns raised by the recent women's rights demonstrations and changes in the law to combat sexual harassment and discrimination and to promote diversity, women in male-dominated careers continue to face an image of incompetence, a lack of voice, a lack of emotional and financial support, barriers to career advancement, and compensation inequities.

The COVID-19 pandemic did not help matters. The stress and

exhaustion of juggling working from home, household chores, and kids home from school forced women to "downshift" their careers, stalling their progression and fueling gender inequality.

More on this subject later.

How can we achieve permanent change and break the Glass Ceiling? The fact is that we need more women in leadership positions to change the male-dominated culture and erase gender inequalities. "Women at the top attract more women at all levels of business… [And] that enterprises with a woman CEO are over 12% more likely to have women as senior general managers…" [9]

Some have suggested that "the trend of women entering predominantly male-dominated fields is steadily rising, so women are out there accepting the challenge, rising to the occasion, and ultimately, making a difference."[10]

But even if there's a trend in the right direction and more businesses are hiring women and minorities for leadership positions, we don't think the workplace is accepting or encouraging these changes. Women and minorities continue to be underrepresented, and the gender pay gap continues to widen.[11]

We must seek support from male colleagues to hire more women into leadership roles while confronting biases. Opportunities should be accessible to deserving individuals in equal numbers, irrespective of gender, race, or any other identity marker. As women, we must display our unique skills and encourage our colleagues and superiors to recognize us and advance our careers. Speaking up for ourselves empowers us. Furthermore, it is crucial to enlighten our male counterparts and superiors on why our collaborations and contributions will enhance the financial success of our employer.

Let's break the Glass Ceiling by overcoming the barriers set to prevent advancement; however, you must be proactive and take responsibility for your growth and development by helping to educate your peers.

Combating Unconscious or Implicit Bias and Gender Discrimination

Glass ceilings are often the result of unconscious bias-instinctive, unintentional beliefs about ethnicity, gender, age, sexuality, social class, or religion—and can become a systemic problem and an inherent part of company culture.[12]

Our brains trigger unconscious (or implicit) bias, automatically making quick judgments of people and situations influenced by our upbringing, personal experiences, societal stereotypes, and cultural context. Gender, race, body weight, age, educational level, social status, disability, accent, and other identifying characteristics can trigger an unconscious bias and lead us to make assumptions about people—even if we don't consciously believe them.[13]

Unconscious biases can manifest in multiple ways, such as during the hiring process, performance evaluations, promotion decisions, and even day-to-day interactions among colleagues, resulting in unequal opportunities, promotional inequities, and pay disparities for specific individuals. Creating homogeneous teams of members with similar backgrounds or characteristics resulting from unconscious biases (which is common) can stifle creativity, innovation, and the exchange of different perspectives, hindering the organization's overall success. These biases perpetuate stereotypes and reinforce societal inequalities, leading to limited opportunities for specific individuals and contributing to a hostile work environment.[14]

To foster cultural change, we must acknowledge and address our unconscious biases and educate our colleagues when we observe them. We cannot influence others to correct their biases if we do not first address our own. For example, typical unconscious biases exercised by men and women include giving challenging projects to men over women or assuming that a pregnant woman will quit her job to care for her family when considering promotions. Unconscious bias can occur in many aspects of the workplace, such as recruitment, promotions, work assignments, evaluations, and more.

These are some common biases you have likely heard: Successful men are perceived as likable and attractive, while successful women are often viewed as unattractive and not likeable. Women are promoted on past achievements, while men get promoted on potential accomplishments.[15] If men "toot their horn" on what they can do, people see them as confident and capable of achievement. Women who do so, in contrast, are viewed as unattractive and unpleasant. "Outspoken" or "loud" women are "too aggressive," "bossy," "bitchy," "not a team player," "can't be trusted," or "too political." Conversely, people view outspoken or "loud" men positively, and their poor behavior is often excused (maybe they are having a bad day or need to raise their voices to force direction). Somehow, that type of immature behavior gains men more respect, and they are seen as strong and confident. A woman who shows emotion or cries is presumed weak and not "cut out to be a leader." However, if she asks for a raise, she is deemed "pushy" and unlikable. This view is not the same for a man. For example, research suggests that women lawyers are more likely to be judged in a harsher light than men when they display assertiveness, self-promotion, or anger, according to University of California at Hastings law professor Joan Williams.[16]

What about women who look out for their peers or subordinates? Most individuals perceive women who help others in the workplace as "motherly," demonstrating maternal behavior often expected of women. Despite their assistance, however, women are less likely to receive extra compensation for their selfless tasks. By contrast, a man who helps others is perceived as "going out of his way" and thus rewarded for his efforts.

The stark reality as a woman is that you are likely to encounter workplace biases daily. For this reason, employers need to remain aware of these prejudices and take steps to actively combat them so that all employees have equal opportunities for success.

Once you understand your own unconscious biases, you can better identify and combat the unconscious biases of others the moment they express them. For example, if you feel that someone is not treating you or someone else fairly, do not be quiet about it; say something. Do so gently and use this moment to educate that person. This will help reduce hostility or defensiveness and foster a positive outcome. The violator may appreciate your feedback. If you are not comfortable addressing the issue in front of others, such as if the violator is in a position of authority or if speaking up would be embarrassing for them, try to find a private moment to speak with the offending party and let them know that their behavior is unacceptable. If this isn't possible, seek out someone who influences the violator and explain your concerns. The goal of intervening in such situations is to ensure that no inappropriate or insensitive comments are allowed to go unchecked. It is crucial to take action and create a culture where everyone feels safe, respected, and heard. If the offensive behavior is especially egregious or continues, it may be time to consult your HR department.

Imagine starting your career in a male-dominated work environment and your male superior informs you that because you are "too pretty" and "his wife might get jealous," you cannot go to an important industry conference attended by company clients, potential business prospects, and your male colleagues. This example is a true story. Was this male superior relying on a legitimate protective work rule to minimize sexual harassment, or was he engaging in blatantly insulting gender discrimination?

A male friend commented on this scenario, "That makes sense to protect the female colleague. Women can't have it both ways. They should not be able to complain about sexual harassment and then object if the company enacts work rules to protect them." But—who are these rules designed to protect, and are they even legal? Is it right to deny a female employee an opportunity at the expense of her career to avoid temptation by a male colleague? Instead, why not educate employees on proper behavior while traveling together on business trips? Education is vital in helping ensure that everyone understands what constitutes appropriate behavior while traveling and the consequences of violating company policies that protect against sexual harassment. Regular reminders reinforce expectations and help create a workplace culture where organizations do not tolerate inappropriate behaviors.

One of the unintended consequences of the #MeToo movement included potential new workplace rules that could ban handshakes or touching of any kind, one-on-one meetings with women behind closed doors, lunches, mentoring, and traveling with a female colleague.

We also heard that some men decided to limit their interactions with women or avoid them altogether. Rep. Robert Foster and former Supreme Court Chief Justice Bill Waller, Jr. have stated that they refused to be alone with a woman who was not their wife, even professionally, citing "common sense" and the "Billy Graham Rule." The late evangelist Billy Graham allegedly stated "that a man cannot be alone with a woman to whom he is not married, including in a professional context." This same issue caused a social media frenzy for VP Mike Pence after a statement he made in 2002 surfaced, stating that he does not eat alone with a woman or attend an event that serves alcohol unless his wife is present.

These supposed "protective" positions and rules are highly prejudicial, counterproductive, and harmful to women's social and professional growth within male-dominated environments. In the workplace, these rules are illegal. Title VII, which governs workplace discrimination, does not allow employers to treat employees differently based on specific protected characteristics, including gender. More importantly, these "protective" positions and rules only underscore the lack of understanding among men of what constitutes gender discrimination and sexual harassment and what is genuinely needed to eliminate discriminatory behavior.

Unfortunately, this failure expands to younger generations of men as well. Would it surprise you to know that in the true story shared above, the superior is in his early thirties? While men may have concerns about being tempted to engage in inappropriate behavior or being perceived as having a sexual relationship if seen alone with a female colleague, it is crucial to ensure that these fears do not prevent women from accessing the same work opportunities as their male counterparts. It is also essential to provide education and training on respectful workplace behavior so everyone can feel protected and respected while traveling together. There are ways to alleviate these fears without eliminating productive business interactions. And, as you might guess, women in the work environment have protected civil rights that far outweigh any spouse-related jealousies or concerns. These biases could threaten female employees' careers and thus must be corrected. Women should not have to suffer because certain male colleagues are not mature enough to control their behavior or are not willing to learn how to respect their female colleagues.

Be aware of the areas where unconscious bias can occur and if you become a target of gender discrimination, consider taking protective measures, such as:

1. Learn about your rights under federal and state laws and company policies on gender discrimination.
   Understand what constitutes gender discrimination, such as unequal pay, harassment, biased hiring, or promotion practices.
2. Keep a record of any instances of discrimination that you experience or witness, including date, time, location, and details of what occurred, preferably not on your work computer. This information can be helpful if you decide to file a complaint or pursue legal action.
3. Speak up and address an inappropriate situation directly with the individual(s) involved. You can also involve a trusted superior who might have influence over the violator(s) or your HR representative. Communicate professionally, clearly expressing

your expectations and desired outcome. Seek support from your allies, such as coworkers, mentors, or professional organizations, to gain support and build a resource network.
4. If you have been the victim of severe gender discrimination and are yet to resolve your concerns, consider seeking legal advice from an attorney or filing a complaint with the appropriate state or federal agency.

Men play an important role in creating a respectful work environment by educating themselves on what constitutes gender discrimination and sexual harassment and how to show respect towards their female colleagues. Ultimately, each individual is responsible for controlling their actions. Everyone can help prevent inappropriate interactions by taking the time to understand appropriate boundaries and behavior in workplaces.

Companies should implement a zero-tolerance policy against discrimination and sexual harassment and provide education on the consequences of violations—a vital step in creating a respectful work environment. It's also critical to guarantee that staff members feel empowered to raise concerns and act promptly and responsibly when they observe inappropriate behavior. Teaching employees how to intervene as bystanders, report incidents, and take other necessary steps can help create a culture where everyone feels safe, respected, and heard.

The statements made by the male superior in the story above about a female worker being too attractive and may serve as a distraction for the males are highly inappropriate and constitute gender discrimination. We are confident his company does not have a policy or work rule specifically prohibiting travel with a female colleague out of concern for potential jealousy from spouses or partners. More importantly, how arrogant is it for the superior to think the female colleague might find him or any of the other male colleagues attractive and want to seek a sexual encounter? Quoting from a recent Vox article, "Employers are not permitted to base employment decisions on gender-based stereotypes—including the stereotype that women are temptresses, or incapable of having purely professional relationships with male bosses or coworkers."[17] It is important to ensure that everyone—male and female—understands appropriate boundaries while traveling and working together so that all colleagues feel safe and respected in their work environment.

In the story above, how can the young female respond respectfully and firmly to her male superior when facing the noted discrimination? She could say, "With all due respect, I am not interested in a personal relationship with anyone at work. I am here to learn and progress in my career. Since this company hired me, I assume it has confidence in my abilities and supports me without prejudice or discrimination. I hope to add value and prove my competence."

While unconscious bias may not be illegal, the actions and decisions it influences can perpetuate workplace discrimination, which *is* unlawful in many jurisdictions.[18] Companies must institute effective policies, procedures, training programs, and diversity initiatives to mitigate unconscious bias and prevent workplace discrimination. Understanding and acknowledging the existence of unconscious bias is essential for creating inclusive and equitable environments. Further, companies should actively train employees to recognize and avoid these biases, as they can lead to unwitting discrimination, negatively impacting employee morale and the health of their organization. Incorporating diversity and inclusion in hiring from the top down regarding race, gender, age, sexuality, education, and social class will allow employees to adapt to the benefits of diversity, including greater collaboration, innovation, enhanced decision-making, improved customer relationships, and fostering personal growth—all while promoting fairness and respect in the workplace.

Men have a critical role to play in creating a safe, respectful work environment free from gender discrimination, sexual harassment, or abuse. Men can create an atmosphere of accountability and encourage positive behavioral change by committing to holding other men to higher standards of behavior and intervening in wrong behaviors when necessary. Companies also need to be transparent about the issue of workplace discrimination and sexual harassment by providing interactive training that focuses on the human element of behavior rather than just technical compliance. Only with these efforts will there be true progress toward creating an environment where everyone is protected against harassment or discrimination.

Dealing with Sexism, Discrimination, and Sexual Harassment

Working in a male-dominated environment can be challenging. It won't be easy to advance if you don't have women with more experience, who are paving the way for you to hold leadership positions and who support your career, or if senior men in your organization aren't committed to elevating women into positions of leadership. We have seen many women throw in the towel and decide to leave a career they worked very hard to earn due to unfair treatment and/or a lack of opportunities, even when qualified. Why put up with constant sexism, discrimination for growth opportunities, and sexual harassment? Eventually, keeping your job does not seem worth the continuous suffering. There is no assurance that leadership will treat you well if you voice your complaints to your supervisor or HR (if your company is big enough to have such a department). You are more likely to be viewed as a "troublemaker," risking future advancement within the company.

The launch of the #MeToo movement sparked renewed conversations regarding sexism, gender discrimination, and sexual harassment. This movement opened doors for women (and men) to share their experiences, causing many old and current violators to face severe consequences, including loss of careers and millions in legal fees/jury verdicts for their employers. Eventually, the movement resulted in a flood of new and updated laws, encouraging companies to implement policies against discrimination and sexual harassment, providing clear procedures for processing claims, regular training and education, and zero tolerance to enforcement for violations, including firing.[19,20]

We have also seen a ban on mandatory arbitration agreements (where employees are required, as a condition to employment, to agree to a private dispute resolution process outside of a court of law) and prohibitions on confidentiality agreements involving settlements of disputes relating to sexual harassment claims. Id.

However, despite these advancements, how many companies have taken action to change their toxic masculine work environments and instances of violative behavior to foster inclusion and growth among their female employees? Statistics from the Equal Employment Opportunity Commission (EEOC) suggest that the number and severity of workplace sexual harassment incidents have not dramatically changed since the launch of the #MeToo movement. For example, sexual harassment charges from 2014 to 2017 accounted for 24.7%, in comparison to 27.7% from 2018 to 2021.[21] Overall, monetary recoveries for sexual harassment claims have increased since the #MeToo movement began. For example, according to the EEOC, in 2021, recoveries were $61.6 million, compared to $46.3 million in 2017.

How long has it been since your organization hit the pause button to check if your workplace has a toxic culture of discrimination, racism, power abuse, and sexual harassment? Do you remember the research conducted by the AllVoices Team on September 1, 2021 noted earlier in this book? According to 832 employees they surveyed, 44% have experienced harassment at work, 38% still experienced harassment remotely, through email, video conferencing, chat apps, or by phone, only 72% believe their workplace wants harassment reported, and 28% say their workplace does not encourage employees to raise issues of harassment.[22]

It would be best to prepare yourself to handle these situations as they arise until your company has implemented effective policies and procedures to address, prevent, and punish inappropriate behavior. Whether you are the target or a bystander of bad behavior, it is crucial to take a stand and address the behavior immediately, calmly yet firmly. Use humor to express your feelings—it can often be an excellent tool for diffusing tense situations. Additionally, organizations should address each incident of inappropriate behavior to educate the wrongdoer on why their actions were unacceptable and to avoid future occurrences of bad behaviors. Many will appreciate such education if you do so kindly and gently. Please read *Play Nice* for more on this subject.

The Boys' Club—Barrier or Opportunity?

Ideally, a woman aiming to succeed in her professional field should not have to face the obstacles an exclusive boys' club poses. However, if you find yourself working in an environment where a boys' club dominates a majority of male colleagues and peers, it may be difficult to ignore the presence of such a group. Know however, that in many cases, the boys' club can provide insight into how men think, strategize, and solve problems, which could prove invaluable for career progression. If your male colleagues view your input as valuable and include you in their conversations, they will likely extend support that could help boost your career prospects further. With that said, it's important to remember that it is ultimately up to you whether you see the boys' club as a barrier or a tool towards progress: use what works best for you! Keep reading for more information about strategies for dealing with the boys' club.

Lack of Mentors and Sponsors for Career Progression

It is often true that to be considered for promotions or other advancement opportunities, having the endorsement and support of a respected sponsor can be incredibly beneficial. This assertion is especially true when there are a lot of other colleagues vying for the same position. To stand out, it is also essential to have a mentor who can guide you through company politics and provide advice on how best to develop your skillset to advance your career. Unfortunately, finding help for your career growth is more challenging if your business does not offer sponsorship or mentorship programs. You will have to take the initiative and seek help from a sponsor or mentor on your own. More on this topic later.

Battling Self Doubt; Insecurities; and Lack of Confidence—Why Women Fail to Toot Their Horn

Women tend to be risk-averse due to a lack of self-confidence and fears of being judged or losing their jobs if they fail, thereby missing opportunities to challenge their abilities, extend beyond their comfort zones, and show-off their strengths to superiors. By comparison, men are typically not risk-averse. Men who fail move on to try again and are not necessarily penalized for failed attempts. Women must speak louder, stand up for themselves, or even express their opinions at work. Some perceive women who speak out or raise their voices as pushy and aggressive. Men, in turn, are more likely to be viewed as confident and deserving of attention for their *perceived* valuable input. Think back to recent meetings or your past classroom experiences. Does this resonate with any incident? How often were you ignored by your fellow male counterparts when you tried to speak up or raise your hand? Some men (and women) have an unconscious bias that men make greater contributions (especially in complicated situations). As a result, their male (and female) superiors call on them more often.

To succeed, women must learn to trust themselves, have faith in their abilities, and be willing to take on challenging opportunities.

Although raising your voice in the workplace may be seen as pushy or aggressive, speaking out with confidence and conviction can lead to better results and greater respect among peers. By understanding the risks associated with taking on personal and professional challenges, women can build resilience, gain experience from potential failure, display their strengths to superiors, empower themselves within the workplace, and even achieve success beyond what they imagined possible. If your male superior ignores you when you raise your hand, find the courage to stand up and say, "It's my turn!" Then, speak what's on your mind about the subject everyone is discussing. Before you know it, the team leader or superior will look at you to see if you have any thoughts or opinions on the subject of discussion.

Now and then, you might question whether you are, in fact, as brilliant as you appear on the outside or just a fraud that is fooling the world. This assertion is known as "Imposter Syndrome," defined by Merriam-Webster as "a psychological condition characterized by persistent doubt concerning one's abilities or accomplishments accompanied by the fear of being exposed as a fraud despite evidence of one's ongoing success." When you start doubting yourself, take inventory of your past successes and reboot. Remember that you are not a fraud and earned the position you hold today through your hard work and dedication. Stop questioning your capabilities, advocate for yourself, and confidently reach for your career goals—you deserve a seat at the table with your peers.

Surround yourself with powerful role models to boost your confidence. Research shows that when women are exposed to powerful female role models, they are more likely to endorse the notion that women are well-suited for leadership roles. So regular meetings—say monthly check-ins or weekly lunches—between less experienced and more senior women give junior women the opportunity to develop professionally and understand that women have what it takes to succeed in an organization's most prestigious roles.[23]

Lack of Transparency; Unequal Pay

As regards women's finances, the glass ceiling limits equal access to opportunities with higher pay.[24]

Then, there is the gender pay gap. Generally, women make up nearly 50 percent of the workforce. Yet, in 2020, they only made 84% of what men earned for the same job. In some states, like Louisiana and Utah, this number is as low as 70 percent.[25] This number dropped even further when considering black women, LGBTQ+ women, and women of color.[26]

The lack of transparency from employers regarding their pay structures makes it significantly more challenging to close the gender pay gap while interviewing for a new job or negotiating a salary increase. Furthermore, this lack of clarity only serves to perpetuate existing systematic disparities between men's and women's wages, continuing to exacerbate the issue at hand. Therefore, employers must make their compensation policies clear and easily accessible so that all potential employees have equal access when making decisions about salaries. It is equally important for existing and potential employees to do their own market research, determining what competitors are paying so they can accurately gauge the actual value of their work. Additionally, individuals should demand transparency from employers regarding pay structures so that everyone has access to the same range of information when making decisions about salaries. This helps both close the gender pay gap and create a more equitable workplace environment.

The Maternity Leave Dilemma

Maternity leave provides mothers with the time they need to recover from childbirth and bond with their newborns. The duration of maternity leave, however, varies by country. Under federal law in the United

States, employees who qualify for The Family and Medical Leave Act of 1993 (FMLA) may be eligible to receive up to 12 weeks of leave without losing their jobs upon their return—*unpaid* leave. To qualify, they must have worked 1,250 hours in the year before their maternity leave with a company with 50 or more employees. The lack of federally mandated paid parental leave in the United States for all employees regardless of company size, signals that it is a privilege, not a right, fostering bias against mothers who choose to take maternity leave. As a result, some supervisors see new mothers as not committed to their jobs or as not likely to return to work. Approximately 44% of all employees—those who work for smaller companies with less than 50 employees, part-time workers, or those who are self-employed, do not qualify for any maternity leave under the FMLA.[27] In contrast, whether a company provides paid maternity leave varies by state. For example, as of 2020, Massachusetts offered the best-paid maternity leave.

In 2019, Massachusetts passed the Massachusetts Paid Family and Medical Leave Act (MA PFML), which grants up to 12 weeks of paid maternity leave to eligible employees. California also has a similar policy.[28]

According to Zippia, only 40% of employers in the U.S. give some form of paid maternity leave, the average being about eight weeks. Id. As a result, only 70% of women take maternity leave, mainly depending on what they can afford. Id. "The U.S. is one of only 4 countries that doesn't offer [federally mandated] paid leave to new mothers—the others are Papua New Guinea, Swaziland, and Lesotho."[29]

President Biden's Build Back Better Act, passed by the U.S. House of Representatives in November 2021, sought to provide all U.S. employees 4 weeks of paid family leave. This Act is now stuck in the Senate.[30]

Women often face the difficult decision of either taking little maternity leave due to financial strain or taking the leave but risk the loss of promotion or even their job if they do not return to work on time.[31]

Paid maternity leave is essential to the health and wellbeing of women and their families. A lack of paid family leave can lead to decreased job stability for both women and men alike due to the pressure placed on one spouse's income following the birth or adoption of a child. "In the U.S., 49% of mothers cobble together paid leave following childbirth using sick days, vacation days, disability leave, and maternity leave." Id. Sadly, paid maternity leave appears to be more prevalent in high-paying jobs. Women who work in low-wage jobs or are self-employed are less likely to have this significant benefit. People who get paid leave are more likely to be affluent, well-educated, and White. U.S. Bureau of Labor Statistics data indicate that about 47% of White parents, 41% of Black parents, and just 23% of Hispanic parents have access to paid leave.[32]

Worse, inadequate or nonexistent childcare options upon returning to work and gender discrimination against working moms add to the stress levels of women in the workforce.

Paid parental leave has been shown to boost productivity levels in the many countries that offer it. This idea reinforces the need for all organizations, regardless of size, to provide more generous policies so mothers (and fathers) may take full advantage of this vital period in their lives and temporarily ensure job security before and after maternity leave. Find out what your company provides in maternity benefits before you embark on your journey to have a family, so you are better prepared and can plan accordingly. I will discuss this issue more in the proceeding chapters of this book.

Lack of Convenient Childcare—
Don't Hang Up Your Career

For working parents, childcare is an important issue. Suppose the employer does not provide affordable daycare on-site or in close proximity. In that case, one or both parental units may be forced to work a limited schedule to accommodate early pick-up requirements or to stay home with their children.

Hiring a full-time nanny can be expensive, especially for the younger parent pool, and extended family assistance may not be available. For nurses, doctors, lawyers, and other professionals requiring long or unpredictable hours, hiring trusting childcare for longer periods of time can be cost-prohibitive and difficult.

Companies that provide accessible childcare to employees can alleviate parental distractions and worries while on the job, fostering a more loyal and productive employee. If this option is not available to you and your job requires you to work late and unpredictable hours, consider workable alternatives before giving up your career. Negotiate the ability to work from home when needed, and resource less expensive childcare options such as students, nurses, or family members who can step in if you cannot pick up from daycare. Take turns with your spouse or partner to care for your children if you work late. Finally, check with colleagues with children, friends, and family for valuable ideas and resources.

2

The Importance of Self-Help in Addressing Obstacles

The Importance of Self-Help Measures in Addressing Obstacles

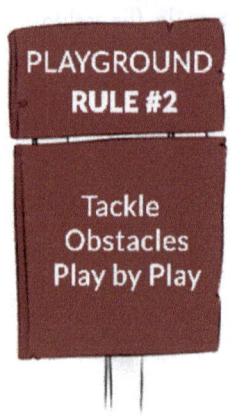

This book shares self-help measures you can use in male-dominated environments to address typical challenges to career progression by using real scenarios experienced by former colleagues, friends, industry executives, and me, including effective advice on tackling these obstacles right when they occur. *Play Nice* uses playground rules to educate your male colleagues and superiors regarding inappropriate behaviors. *Play Smart* continues this concept by adding playground rules to help you develop habits to conquer everyday challenges as you progress in your career.

It's up to us women, and men and women holding leadership positions within companies, to defend against, redirect, and modify toxic and discriminatory behaviors. It's up to us women to recognize, improve, and use our unique skills to advance our careers and educate our male counterparts

The Importance of Self-Help in Addressing Obstacles

and superiors on why our contributions are valuable to improving company performance. We must develop self-awareness, practice critical thinking skills, understand biases, and recognize potential obstacles. This way, we can be better prepared to succeed in our workplaces. Taking initiative with self-help measures is essential in reaching these goals.

First, we must establish personal boundaries, enforce them confidently and correctly, encourage dialogue for support, promote accountability, and foster corrective action.

Establish Your Boundaries

You must establish and communicate your boundaries properly, firmly and politely. Addressing the bias directly and promptly when the issue arises allows women to assert their boundaries and clarify that such behavior is unacceptable. You do not have to be rude. Be gentle and respectful, and use a little humor if appropriate. Defending yourself against the bias calmly and competently can be highly effective. You are more likely to be heard and appreciated for showing the offender a better way. For example, if someone touches sensitive spots of your body without your permission (rubbing your shoulders or legs or putting their arm around your waist or neck), steps into your comfort zone, tells inappropriate jokes thinking you might like them, talks inappropriately about another female in the group, or leaves you an inappropriate personal communication as a joke to see how you will react, respond immediately to establish your boundary. Some easy responses include standing up and saying, "Hey, take a step back; you are in my personal space, and that makes me uncomfortable." "Hey, no touching allowed! That is not in my job description." "Hey, no nasty jokes, please (or comments about our lady colleagues) (or nasty drawings); they make me uncomfortable." Add: "If someone sees your behavior, they may report you to HR, and I don't want you to get into trouble!"

Taking Action Builds Confidence

Confronting the issue yourself can help women build confidence and assertiveness in dealing with difficult situations. The more you tackle unwelcome behavior, the more your assertiveness will become second nature, and your confidence will grow. For example, speak up if a colleague or superior asks you to perform a task below your pay grade and you know there are other persons more appropriate for the job; smile and say that you do not want to miss important aspects of the meeting having to fetch coffee, making copies or taking notes. Propose that it might be more beneficial for the group's administrative assistant to handle such tasks. Then, coordinate for them to step in and complete the requested task.

Foster Dialogue for Support

Your confidence to speak up will encourage much-needed open dialogue. Directly addressing the issue can open up new and meaningful conversations and create an opportunity for education, awareness, or change. More importantly, your male colleagues will appreciate and respect you more for teaching them better ways to behave rather than getting them in trouble with HR. For example, since my retirement from the practice of law, I joined my husband and his former work colleagues, all great male friends, for an almost weekly Mexican lunch on Fridays. Over the years, this group has been a great sounding board and resource for many topics related to *Play Nice* and *Play Smart*. For example, you might expect off-color comments, jokes, or stories to be told at a mostly male lunch involving margaritas! If the group sees me stand up or raise my finger, they know they have said something inappropriate. They will either immediately apologize and correct themselves or ask me to explain why their comment or behavior was not appropriate. We also spend time talking about the latest news stories that showcase bad behavior and potential consequences. Over time, they have become much more knowledgeable about bad behavior and even occasionally bring their daughters to share and discuss their work experiences.

Promote a Culture of Accountability

Your assertiveness will promote a culture of accountability. By addressing bad behaviors directly, women can create a culture where everyone is accountable for their actions, fostering a more respectful work environment. For example, raising true occurrences of discrimination in an open forum with management present can foster positive discussion, an action plan on handling bad behavior in the future, and a commitment to hold the violator accountable.

Foster Corrective Action

Most importantly, your efforts will likely prompt corrective actions. Addressing the problem immediately can lead to a quicker resolution, preventing further harm and promoting a healthier work environment. Your male colleague will learn a valuable lesson and hopefully appreciate your efforts to protect him from the wrath of HR. If he forgets and slips back to bad behavior, all you have to do is raise your finger and remind him of your last discussion. He should immediately remember, and hopefully, you will get an apology and an affirmation not to repeat such behavior.

However, if your gentle self-help efforts fail with a person or group of violators and they insist on ignoring your attempts to educate them, seek the help of a superior to correct the situation on your behalf. If the superior is not successful, it's time to visit HR. Ensure you have documented all instances sufficiently in detail and recruit a few witnesses to help support your complaint.

The goal of *Play Smart* is to empower you to become bolder, fuel your confidence, help you foster trust, and create better work relations with your male colleagues in the sandbox of the workplace playground—to open doors for your career and make your path to success as healthy and fruitful as possible. With a deeper understanding of the typical obstacles and equipping yourself with the right tools to combat them, you can strive for success more confidently.

3

Our Playground Rules for Success

Learn the Rules of the Sandbox; Be Ready and Prepared to Play, Take Your Job Seriously, Be Invested in Your Job

If you don't ask questions or take action, you don't gain. It is that simple. As women, we often hear, "Just keep your head down, mind your own business, and work hard; you will eventually receive the reward for your hard work." While this can be beneficial, in my opinion, "eventually" more often means *"maybe you will be rewarded."* If the opportunity presents itself, you should do more and go the extra mile. Understand your work environment, including your company's business, clients, and industry. Stand up for yourself for all to hear you positively. Taking risks, seeking growth opportunities, challenging yourself, and asking for promotions are positive elements for career progression. Women are not always comfortable conducting these actions, but these steps are essential for your growth and success.

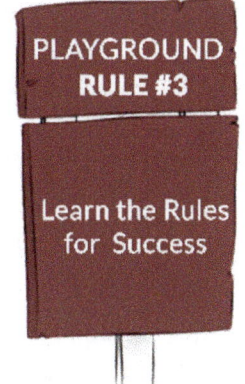

Understand Your Company's Business, Industry and Customers

Before you interview with the company and start your job, research as much as you can about the structure and composition of the company. Who founded the company? How old is the company? What is the company's primary goal and purpose? Who are the company's customers? What are the company's divisions, and how would you fit in with your work experience or qualifications? Where would your expertise add value, or where would you learn the most? Does the company have a positive work culture? Is there a path for career progression? Knowing more about the company shows that you are genuinely interested in working for them, depicting you as a more attractive hire. Superiors want to foster and promote growth with employees who show more interest and invest their time and energy in the company. You will not last very long or accelerate in your field if you are just there to collect a paycheck.

Once you have joined the company, understand your job expectations and responsibilities. Know relevant things like how your division operates and what behavior they reward. What is the culture of the division concerning working hours (including on the weekends and working remotely), work attire, and social gatherings? Get to know colleagues who are more senior as a resource for important information. Introduce yourself to executives and leadership, keeping an eye out for resourcing sponsors and mentors for advice and future growth opportunities. More on this later.

You will appear to be an interested and noteworthy employee by asking engaging and important questions.

As a new hire, your company has invested in you, so you should do the same. Roll up your sleeves and get to work!

Understand your company's business model, purpose, and vision, including its products, industry markets, customers, and strategies. If you are seeking new business, research your target and understand how your company and its products, business, or advisors will add value—learn how to sell your company and the expertise of your division.

Take advantage of relevant seminars and educational classes to stay on top of your job responsibilities. Knowledge is power and will make you a better expert in your field. Understand your role and how you can best achieve expectations. All these will not happen overnight; however, remember that information and preparedness are potent assets enabling you to contribute to conversations and projects with confidence and influence, ultimately fostering your career. These actions will also help you become an important resource for your colleagues and a valued employee.

Personal Development. Building Credibility: Be a Team Player; Roll Up Your Sleeves; Dig In; Be Flexible

Being a team player is essential to succeed in your job. Understanding your role and responsibilities within the team and those of other members is also beneficial. Learning each team member's job responsibilities from the bottom to the top will make you a more effective leader. All you need to do is invest enthusiastically in the work and offer necessary support, take ownership of your tasks passionately, and strive to learn quickly. People will notice your hard work and will likely notice you, leading to faster career progression.

I still remember early in my career when a law partner told me to be sure our closing documents were complete, accurate, adequately organized, and bound professionally without tears, typos, or missing exhibits. Sounds trivial, right? It was late at night after two weeks of negotiating and revising closing documents for the sale of an office building. Our transaction had finally been consummated, and to our superior, the binders containing the final signed documents of the sale were the most important part of the transaction. Before sending them to the client, we spent hours ensuring the binders and related documents were perfect. "You are only as good as the last deal you closed," our superior would say. "There is nothing worse than your client needing a copy of a closing document and finding out that it is incomplete, missing exhibits, or flawed with errors. Your sloppy work might risk your reputation and ability to be hired for the next transaction.

Our superior was correct. Your attention to detail regardless of the task positively affects how you are perceived by your company and your client. You should always strive for perfection at every turn, as even the slightest mistake could damage your reputation and put future deals at risk, not only for yourself, but for your team and company. Creating a perfect closing binder might seem like a menial task; however, in the legal profession, its condition could impact the receipt of future work. Worse, mistakes in the closing documents could risk future litigation.

As a young attorney, I made every effort to learn all the various aspects of my job and what it takes to close a deal successfully, including all of the necessary support functions (from making copies of closing documents to mastering computer programs needed to generate important documents and data). I endeared myself to the staff tasked with important closing functions so I could understand their work challenges (especially when given tight deadlines) and got to know the various departments whose help was required to meet important expectations. These seemingly menial functions were critical to support our job responsibilities as attorneys (developing closing strategies, negotiating terms, crafting the closing documents, and promoting smooth dealings with closing parties to complete transactions successfully).

To become a good leader, you must roll up your sleeves, dive in deep, and understand all facets of the job from start to finish. You can't necessarily go home at night if members of your team are still working hard to accommodate task deadlines. Your superiors, colleagues, and staff want to know that you care about them and the company. The same goes for your customers, clients, and their transactions. Make sure you are adding value with your contributions. Your client or customer should feel like they and their transaction are your priority. You will need your team members to support your efforts accordingly. Compliance and coordination among your team is critical for success.

Additionally, first impressions count. Decide what you want your reputation to be and work to achieve it. Understand that women generally must work harder to earn respect and overcome workplace stereotypes—especially in a male-dominated profession. Be cautious and aware, as you may not necessarily realize stereotypes are being applied to you.

If you become a solid contributor with a reliable reputation early in your career, your hard work is more likely to pay off later—for example, if you desire accommodations, such as a more flexible work schedule for a period of time as you start a family.

When I started my first job, I was not married and did not have children. I worked late hours and rarely said "no" to new projects. I developed a reputation as a very reliable hard worker who produced solid work for our firm's clients. When I later got married and had children, my reputation as a valuable quality contributor remained despite adjusting my work schedule. I will discuss the challenges of juggling family and personal time later in this book.

Don't Skip Meetings

Going to meetings is very beneficial, especially if organized by your superiors. It increases your visibility in the company, allows you to be heard by colleagues and superiors, and provides a platform for networking with others in your field, which can lead to new opportunities. Meetings are a great way to share and gather information, stay up-to-date on industry developments, and learn from others. Participating in meetings gives you a voice in decision-making. It enhances your professional development, allowing you to showcase your skills and work expertise.

Pay Attention and Take Notes

Whether in a planning session, at a lunch meeting, or another event with clients or colleagues, taking notes is essential for capturing important information that might be useful later on. You may need to reference the information later, or you may gain important advice to help build your career. Additionally, if anything needs to be solved during the meeting, take ownership and research potential resolutions to share when you meet next. This proactive attitude may even earn you positive recognition from your peers. Moreover, your colleagues and clients will be impressed if you remember things that are important to them. Show that you care about your clients or customers by building a close relationship with them for marketing purposes. Ensure you remember the names of their children, where they are from, their favorite teams and hobbies, and other interests. When you see them again, taking the time to ask them about these personal matters will leave a good impression and help foster an even closer bond between both of you.

Understand Your Assignments, Set Expectations, and Ask for Feedback

Get to know the senior folks assigning you projects. If it is your first time working for someone, visit with others who have worked with that same person and understand what they look for in style and contribution. This way, you can present your work in an expected format to avoid mistakes others have made. Ensure you understand the scope of the assignment and expectations regarding substance, goals, format, notation of any resources, and the timing for completion. Ask for clarification if there is any confusion.

Once your project is complete, request feedback and be open to constructive criticism. Ask specific questions like "Is there anything I should do more of? Anything I should stop doing? Am I on the right track?" These questions demonstrate you're interested in improving your performance and care about receiving honest feedback. Not only will this allow you to understand whether or not you met expectations, but it also provides a valuable opportunity to grow as an employee by considering any suggestions offered by those evaluating your work.

Learn How to Delegate for Success as Appropriate

As your workload increases and you have difficulty keeping up, delegate portions of your work where appropriate and as permitted. Training someone new to help you may seem daunting and time-consuming, but it is an invaluable opportunity to further your career. It helps you to learn and develop management skills. By delegating tasks effectively, not only do you free up more time for yourself to handle more important tasks, but you also train a team member who will be able to help you and your team with future projects or assignments. These efforts can be especially beneficial if the tasks require specialized knowledge that you need to complete the project.

Mentoring and training subordinates and colleagues are essential to fostering a successful workplace. Not only will you be providing invaluable opportunities for others, but you'll also be laying the foundation to build your own team while increasing profitability and the overall value of the company. Through this process, not only will your business base expand, but also your share of profits from such growth through a potential increase in pay, bonuses, and/or job promotion.

Don't Give Anyone a Reason to Challenge Your Abilities; Be Prepared and Produce Quality Work Product

When a superior welcomed me to his team as the only female, he noted, "This team works hard, including late at night and on the weekends, so you will have to buck up since women can't perform like men." I smiled at his comment and replied, "Thank you for the opportunity. I look forward to proving you wrong!" And I did. I made sure my work was top quality by going the extra mile. For years, when I completed projects, he would complement my work, and I would make comments like, "Not bad for a woman, huh?" Or, "Running circles around my male colleagues, aren't I?" Remembering our first meeting, he would laugh at my comments. I agree with Megyn Kelly's view regarding "hard work matters" in her book *Settle for More*. "It's not that I reject the idea of demanding a place at the table—quite the contrary. But in my experience, the most effective way to get opportunities is with performance, not persistence. Hard work matters. I so much believe that."[1]

First and foremost, hard work is important. However, you must also speak up for yourself and be persistent in receiving acknowledgment for your accomplishments.

I grew up in a military family where my parents taught me that if I worked hard to achieve with poise and confidence, my work, attitude, and dedication would be noticed and subsequently rewarded. They also taught me never to give anyone a reason to criticize my work or my abilities, demonstrating that I must always add value to the task, team, client, and company.

However, if you are not recognized for your contributions despite your strong work effort, respectfully demand to be acknowledged. When you have a strong reputation and produce high-quality work, your superiors will find it hard to deny you the opportunity to sit at the table.[2] Your success is in your own hands, so don't miss out on this chance!

Work Hard

As I noted, working hard is important. However, hard work doesn't just mean working long hours or delivering your work product on time.

It means taking ownership, understanding your assignment, working with attention to detail, thinking critically about strategies and solutions, producing top-quality work while keeping any objectives (meaning the big picture) in mind, and completing the assignment with efficiency in accordance with expectations. It also means promptly following up to correct or supplement, if required, following feedback from your superiors.

Knowledge is Power; Do Your Research

The importance of knowledge and preparation cannot be understated. Before imploring your seniors with questions, ensure you have done all the necessary research to find an answer. When completing projects, do so to the best of your ability; laziness will only result in a negative perception from your superiors. One of my favorite associates once handed me a final report, saying, "I am 95% sure that my report is accurate." I don't think he meant to say that out loud. Still, his comment caused concern, and I became worried about the previous work he had completed. If there are any lingering doubts or concerns about accuracy or completeness, don't hesitate to voice these concerns before you complete your project. Your superior may be able to help you address them for 100% accuracy. By backing up opinions and conclusions with reliable and thorough facts, you demonstrate intellect, reliability, and concern for the topic at hand—traits that will give you important credibility. Admitting to 95% accuracy might risk your career growth.

Learn From Prior Transactions

Studying similar transactions your company has already worked on can be an excellent resource for current projects. Doing so allows you to minimize inefficiency and find areas of improvement that will draw positive attention to your work. Analyzing previous efforts is an effective way to move ahead in the game and ensure you deliver only the best results.

Learn How to Add Value, Foster Respect, Confidence and Reliability

Preparing for a project or discussion is essential to ensure you are knowledgeable on the topic and able to provide meaningful input. Make sure you research beforehand to understand the nuances and counterarguments related to the subject matter and any open issues that need resolving. Not only will this garner your superiors' respect and trust in your work ethic, but it will also equip you with informed questions and potential resolutions. This way, you can contribute confidently during discussions rather than taking shortcuts or relying solely on others for solutions.

When presenting your ideas or alternate solutions, back them up with relevant data and evidence so people can decide what would work best for everyone involved. This way, all parties will recognize and appreciate your efforts in the project or discussion. Most importantly, take every opportunity to learn from people within and outside of your team. Get out of your comfort zone. Building solid relationships with colleagues in other departments can help you better understand your company's various needs and challenges. Taking the initiative and going beyond what is required to educate yourself and others on important topics of interest can also increase your value, allowing you to develop into a reputable person that others would love to listen to. So, when it comes to critical decisions or discussions of your organization, don't be afraid to raise your hand or speak up—the organization will take you seriously because you've earned it, and now that others recognize you as an expert on specific subjects.

My father used to tell me that if you work for a difficult superior or client, find a way to add value and earn that person's trust and respect.

"Work hard to become an expert in your area of work." "Knowledge is power." Also, learn to "make your superior look good in the eyes of others" instead of demeaning their intelligence. That last one was especially important for JR and me in our respective professions. Never correct your superior or client or make that person look bad in front of others. The preceding applies to female clients and superiors as well. It's even better to "manipulate that person into thinking your idea was his or hers." A few of my father's famous words. JR calls it "stroking" the client or superior or "working JR's magic." No man wants a female to "boss him around" or "correct his opinion on a matter—especially in front of others."

Interestingly, men can do that to other men all day and not appear offended. JR and I are known as calm, levelheaded negotiators who can make difficult parties compromise with tact and patience. We both learned how to add value and complement the strengths and weaknesses of our counterparts. We learned how to modify behavior and engender respect for ourselves and the female members of our teams. We both became successful in our professions and became preferred hires—especially by our male clients. More later on why women are beneficial and add value to the workforce.

Be True to Your Word; Be Reliable; Follow Through with Commitments

It's important always to follow through when you commit to a task. Please do so to maintain your reputation, as it will only reflect poorly on you and your team if you don't. If the due date becomes unrealistic or you need more information to complete the assignment, ensure that the assigning parties are aware of this as soon as possible. Communication should be a two-way street. Ask your delegators to inform you of any changes or developments necessary to complete your project. Keep your delegators updated on all progress made and provide regular updates on where you are with the project. Also, ensure the assigning parties have enough time to review your project once it is complete in case changes are needed before any deadlines to deliver the final product to clients.

Always be aware of your strengths and weaknesses, and never give anyone a reason to doubt your abilities. Seek help when obstacles beyond your control appear so you can rise above them quickly. Establish yourself as someone who can be counted on by consistently delivering quality results on time—this will help build trust in the workplace and open doors for future successes. Finally, don't forget to recognize the value of your contributions—understanding the impact of what you do can make all the difference!

Managing Deadlines and Expectations— Don't Be Afraid to Say "No" Nicely

Sometimes, you may have multiple work projects with competing deadlines from superiors who all claim their project has priority. As an attorney, this happened to me frequently. I would already be working late to satisfy deadlines when another partner would throw an additional assignment on my desk for completion in short order. It did not matter that I was already working late or the superior had other available associates. Initially, I was worried that responding: "Sorry, I already have a full plate!" would harm my reputation and earn a bad review from the applicable partner. So, I did what I could (even working all night) to finish all the competing projects on time. My goal was always to be a team player and never give anyone a reason to doubt my willingness to work. Eventually, when my workload became too overwhelming potentially risking the quality of my work product, I finally asked a superior colleague for help. He recommended that I be bold but gentle by providing complete transparency to my superiors regarding the competing work and deadlines. A recent article from The Muse made an important point concerning this matter:

"It's all too easy to say yes to every project as you strive to "be a good employee"—but if you never say no, you'll ultimately just hurt yourself and your company. It's important to stand up for the projects you so desire to work on...., and then push back at other times when you don't have the capacity. You can bet many guys say no—and you should, too."[3]

If you think the due date for the assignment is unrealistic or you already have competing deadlines, inform the assigning superiors to communicate and resolve the deadline requirements among themselves. Additionally, have your superiors establish a list of priorities and realistic deadlines so you can complete each project within a reasonable timeline. If one or more of your superiors are unwilling to cooperate, seek the assistance of a more senior person for how you might resolve the conflicts.

For example, one of my senior partners at my law firm (we call him John) was never willing to accept that I was working on competing projects. If there was a timing issue, I learned to say, "Let me check with [Peter] to see if his deadline has some flexibility, and I will let you know what he says." If Peter did not have flexibility, he would call or visit with John to work out a timeline or ask John to find another person to work on the project.

If you are bold enough to say, "I already have a conflict concerning your deadline," when the new project is assigned, be sure to add that you are willing to take on the assignment if the due date is flexible, and if not, that you would like to work on their next project. If you know someone who can take on the project, suggest them. Be helpful and resourceful, if possible, to leave a positive impression. The superior may experience pressure from clients to complete a project under similar deadlines, and your superior will likely appreciate your proposal for alternative assistance. As soon as you have free time, go back to that superior and find out if you can do anything to help them. It is always imperative to work through competing deadlines to manage expectations, no matter how uncomfortable this effort may seem.

Address Disagreements Head On

When conflicts arise, approach them directly without pointing fingers, being defensive, or acting confrontational—especially when communicating with a superior. If you need to calm down, take a break for a walk or for coffee, talk to a friend or colleague, and refrain from sending angry emails. Remember, written communication is permanent and can harm your reputation. If you get an unpleasant email, refrain from responding through email; try to resolve the issue in person while remaining calm and positive. If the problem is sensitive, bring a witness along. Once you resolve the conflict, don't hold any grudge. Earning your colleague's respect is crucial for future cooperation.

Acknowledging You Made a Mistake

Managing a team is tough. The leader or head of the project is ultimately responsible for the team's work, including any mistakes made. If you discover you or a team member made an error, be honest and address it immediately with your superior. However, before you point out the mistake, get the error fixed. If it's too late, collaborate and implement new processes that will prevent the error from occurring again. Honesty and transparency are the best ways to recover from a misstep. "When you bring up a weak performance in the right way, you'll prove to your boss that you're proactive, committed to quality work, and ready and willing to do what you need to improve. And if you take your manager's feedback to heart, you'll avoid repeat performances in the future."[4]

Your superior will want to know that you and your team members are meeting your respective responsibilities.

We recently spoke to a group of employees hired for a startup company. Each was hired to fulfill a role and was assumed to have the necessary qualifications to complete expected responsibilities. Growth for the small company came fast. It did not take long for certain employees to become overwhelmed with job duties beyond what they were assigned, while other employees were completing assignments without the proper experience, guidance, and supervision—leading to inevitable mistakes. Remember, the buck stops with you if you are the manager in charge. Hire, manage and train accordingly.

Welcome Constructive Feedback

Providing or receiving constructive feedback on a work-related matter can be daunting and difficult for both parties. If you are on the receiving end, feedback is critical to improving your skills, knowledge, work product, and relationships at work and to helping you satisfy job expectations going forward.[5]

You may neither like nor respect the messenger, but don't be defensive. Being defensive when receiving important feedback risks losing valuable insight into resolving obstacles to your career growth.

If you receive unsolicited feedback, stay calm, take a deep breath, and listen carefully without interrupting. Take notes and ask for clarification if necessary. Avoid overanalyzing or questioning the person's assessment. Give them the benefit of the doubt. They obviously thought it was necessary to provide the feedback. Before you leave, make sure you have repeated for confirmation a summary of the corrective actions to be taken and thank them for taking the time to speak with you.

If you have asked for feedback, appreciate that the provider is taking time out of their schedule to evaluate your work. Listen without interruption, take notes, and ask clarifying questions to understand the constructive feedback better. Discuss what you can do to avoid any criticisms in the future. Once finished, commit to the noted changes, and thank them for their time and efforts.

Learn From the Good and the Bad

Strive to treat each coworker respectfully, regardless of their feelings. Look for the positives in every interaction and use what you learn to empower your work style. At the same time, be mindful to avoid emulating any negative habits they may possess. Bad work habits that co-workers have can be very damaging to workplace dynamics and productivity. Examples of bad work habits include:

- ✓ Being chronically late.
- ✓ Not taking the initiative on tasks.
- ✓ Engaging in gossip or unprofessional conversations.
- ✓ Procrastinating instead of tackling projects head-on.
- ✓ Failing to communicate important information effectively with colleagues.
- ✓ Not following through on agreements or commitments made to the team.
- ✓ Wasting time by browsing social media during working hours.

Avoid these behaviors to ensure a thriving work environment free from hostility and negative perceptions.

Keep a Positive Attitude

Yes, there will be moments where you wish you could erase all troubling encounters. You will be working with all types of personalities, including people who are loud, rude, and known bullies. Most companies have them. With any luck, in advance, your colleagues will warn you about these folks and give you tips on how to best deal with them. If you have one or more negative experiences, try not to take their behavior personally. Stay positive, but don't let the bully compromise who you are. Suppose challenging encounters become too frequent or you have become a bully's regular target; in such a case, it is time to seek help from a superior or HR.

Focus on the Positives if your Project Outcome Fails

Approaching work challenges with a positive attitude can lead to valuable learning experiences, even when faced with criticism for unexpected outcomes. It's important to uplift yourself and your team during these times to foster growth and resilience. For example, if your team did not complete a project on time, provide a positive review, such as "Despite the late arrival of critical data for completion, the recent corporate restructuring causing the project to be understaffed, and a deadline that should have been at least 5 weeks later given market challenges, our skeletal staff did an excellent job completing the project ahead of what would have been a more reasonable deadline." Try your best to be upbeat and educational, acknowledging your team's challenges. A favorable spin will help build morale and set a positive tone with superiors who might have to justify any perceived failures to their superiors.

Keep Communications Professional—Limit Personal Information

It is important to be mindful of the information you share with your superiors and colleagues, especially regarding challenges in your personal life. Keeping specific topics private can help ensure that stress-related issues are not misinterpreted as signs of weakness or incompetence in the workplace. Instead, focusing on discussing positive experiences and successes may make your superior more likely to entrust you with challenging projects and responsibilities.

Be Informative, Succinct, and Direct

Be prepared before you report on a project, seek clarification on tasks to be completed, or enter a brainstorming session with superiors. Your communications should be informative, direct, and concise. Avoid being long-winded or straying off-topic. Show that you value your audience's time by being thoughtful about what you have to say so they can see the effort you put in ahead of time.

Negotiating Skills and Conflict Resolution

Read up on different negotiation strategies and tactics, such as splitting the difference, concession trading, principled negotiation, and win/win solutions. Attend meetings where superiors make the deals to help you determine what makes negotiators successful. Watch their body language, tone of voice, and tactics to understand their strategy. Interview them later to learn more about their desired outcome for the meetings, if their goals for the meetings were met, and what they might have done differently. Often negotiations can be quite challenging, and compromises must be made to accommodate changes in outcomes. Learning from more senior men and women in our respective fields of work was very valuable for JR and me.

Learn active listening. It's essential in any conversation, but especially in negotiations, that you pay attention not only to what someone says but also learn how to interpret unspoken cues and signals they may be sending out. Learning active listening will help you pick up on nuances that could be beneficial during your negotiations, allowing both parties involved to get more out of the discussion than had been initially expected or thought possible.

Understand precisely what outcome best serves your interests and be prepared to compromise. There will likely need to be some give-and-take between both sides. So, while it's important to have a clear idea before beginning talks, be ready and willing (within reason) to adapt if necessary and find an agreement with which both parties are happy to achieve successful outcomes.

Most importantly, anticipate contentious topics and be prepared to offer solutions and ways to compromise. In a tense situation, seek to be the calming influence. You could suggest taking a break and getting coffee before regrouping to discuss contentious topics. Take time to list out all of the issues in dispute and understand both sides' perspectives on them. Explain why certain points are problematic from your side, providing examples if necessary. Propose solutions that accommodate everyone's interests without compromising either side so you can move toward a positive outcome. In my time as a lawyer, my clients often asked me to address difficult topics and suggest ways to resolve them with the other side in advance of meetings to help the discussions run amicably. My calm demeanor and gentle communication style were often beneficial in easing tensions after heated discussions between the parties. Understanding the concerns of both sides and finding solutions that do not compromise either of their positions is a very valuable skill to learn.

Be Organized and Professional

How you dress, handle yourself, keep your office, and craft your work product is an extension and a reflection of who you are. First impressions are crucial. For many workplaces, the work environment has changed to a much more casual and flexible setting; however, it is still important to pay special attention to the tone and culture of your office, including any etiquette, code of conduct, and dress code protocols. In most cases, your company's principals have worked very hard to build a successful company with a positive reputation for their brand. They expect you to help them shine and continue fostering the company's reputation and success. Being ignorant of your office culture and code of conduct will harm your career—the same with being disrespectful. For example, ask about appropriate attire if a superior invites you to a meeting or lunch with a client. Take these opportunities seriously and don't be unprofessional. You are attending the meeting or lunch as a representative of the company.

Your Office or Workspace

It's important to stay consistent with the values and standards set by your employer when personalizing your workspace. Additionally, consider the impact of any decorations you choose, ensuring they are not distracting or overly disruptive for colleagues who use shared office spaces. When selecting items such as plants, paintings, or prints on posters, think about what message it sends out about yourself and whether it's appropriate for an office environment. Personalizing your office with accessories is acceptable; however, remember that how you decorate reflects on your personality and in part, your company. Your office design is critical, especially if you are hosting meetings or are on regular video conference calls. Consider the following:

Step back and look at your workspace and decor with fresh eyes.

If you work from home, avoid using pictures or decorations that might be too personal, controversial, or offensive. Conversation starters are fine, especially if they are positive (such as a picture of your favorite charity activity, college colors, or a special award you may have received).

Keep your area, space, or office clean. This will give the impression of being organized, paying attention to details, and "on top of your game."

For example, at my first job, I decided to give a new hire from another law firm the lead on a new project. Her desk was barely visible, filled with disorganized stacks of paper. Worse, she had more stacks of legal files, paper, and books lying around on the floor with old "to-go" bags of food on top of them. As I made room to sit on a chair with more files, I asked if she had reviewed the background transaction documents for the matter I was delegating to her. "Yes," she said as she ruffled through her stacks of paper for several minutes to locate them.

She failed my first impression. Even though we had set a time, she was not prepared for our meeting. The disarrayed state of her office made me wonder whether she was the right person for the project.

Would she be able to prioritize and complete the transaction in a timely manner? Would her work product look accurate and professional to her superiors and the client? I was worried.

Even if you are the most hardworking and dedicated employee, a messy workspace can jeopardize your efforts and reputation. Our new, messy employee needed constant prodding and supervision to meet our client's deadlines. Because of this, she did not become a permanent addition to our firm.

Your Work Product

Before you start a project, it's essential to understand the assignment and any associated goals or objectives. Take the time to research your concerns before asking questions of the assigning party and, if necessary, solicit advice from others who have worked for the same superior. Pursuing this path can help you learn what they look for when completing projects. However, remember that while asking questions is okay, try not to rely on getting spoon-fed needed information. Instead, take initiative and don't be afraid to think through components of tasks yourself as part of your preparation. Once you've done this, outline how to complete the task, and get to work. Complete the project to the very best of your ability, timely, efficiently and professionally (well organized, with proper supporting back up, and without typos and grammatical errors). Remember, your work product reflects your talents, abilities and your value to the company. Then, ask for feedback.

Step Out of Your Comfort Zone—If You Are Not Busy, Ask for Work

If you are not busy at work, check with your colleagues to see if anyone needs help. Offering your services has several benefits, such as promoting collaboration and cooperation among team members and fostering a positive work environment. You show that you are a team player and willing to support your colleagues by providing assistance. These actions can lead to stronger relationships with your coworkers and create a sense of camaraderie within the workplace. Lastly, helping others can enhance your skills and knowledge, demonstrate your value as an employee, and help with career advancement and job security.

Work Outside Your Section or Group

Working outside your section or group at work helps you gain exposure to different teams and projects, develop new skills, and broaden your network within the company. It can also demonstrate your willingness to help others and take on new challenges, improving your reputation and career advancement opportunities. If you want to increase your knowledge and strengthen your skillset:

- ✓ Take the initiative to reach out to individuals you have yet to collaborate with.
- ✓ Let them know you are open to new opportunities and can work with them on a project.
- ✓ Make it a weekly habit to look for new people interested in teaming up with you.

Your offers to help or collaborate will create strong impressions of proactivity and dedication, which, in turn, could result in support for rewards such as promotions or salary raises—even if you never actually worked with the person supporting you.

Challenge Your Abilities, Volunteer for Difficult Tasks

Challenging your abilities and volunteering for complex tasks at work can help you grow professionally and personally. Pushing yourself beyond your comfort zone can help you develop new skills, gain valuable experience, and demonstrate your capabilities to your colleagues and superiors. Additionally, taking on challenging tasks can show your dedication and commitment to your job, leading to opportunities for advancement and increased responsibilities in the future. Challenging yourself by volunteering for complex tasks can help you build confidence, improve your performance, and ultimately achieve your career goals.

Manage Your Position on the Team—Ask for What You Want—Set Project-Based Goals

As you mature through your company's ranks, pay attention to upcoming projects and other areas of work that can facilitate your growth. Act boldly and ask if you can participate in these endeavors. Be firm, direct, and straightforward when offering help. You could say, "I would love to work with you on the upcoming project. It is exactly in my field of interest, and I am ready for this challenge!" Even if your superior denies you the opportunity to participate in a particular project, they will never forget your initiative of asking, increasing your likelihood of being sought out for future opportunities.

Take on More Responsibility; Take on Leadership Roles

"Sadly, most bosses are too busy to figure out the most equitable project allocation, and it often comes down to who yapped last to them about that hot media deal or the new partnership your company is launching. If you aren't good at grabbing your boss in the hall or during your morning coffee break and bringing up the projects that excite you, then schedule a formal time to check in at least once a month and let your boss know what you'd like to work on."[6]

Leadership roles offer you valuable opportunities for personal and professional growth. Additionally, they can help you build important communication, collaboration, problem-solving, and decision-making skills, which will be helpful for you throughout your career.

If you are offered a leadership role, whether on a project or a subject matter important to your company, accept it. If you see a project that needs leadership, take charge of it. Don't wait for someone else to take the opportunity. If you notice a recurring topic of interest among your colleagues, conduct the research and become the go-to person with the most expertise to foster credibility and respect. Take the opportunity to step out of your comfort zone.

Accepting a leadership role demonstrates confidence in your capabilities and shows you are willing to take on challenges. As a leader, you can influence others' work and decisions while impacting the team or organization at large. Your efforts are likely to open doors to more senior positions with increased responsibilities and rewards.

Develop Goals for Your Future

Has anyone ever asked you, "Where would you love to see yourself in your career in the next five to ten years from now?" Having long-term goals is essential for achieving success and satisfaction in any career. It's important to break down those objectives into near—, intermediate—, and far-term goals so you can chart a path toward the future of your dreams. Not only should these be written out as achievable milestones, but it can also be helpful to create visuals and sketches of what each goal looks like when achieved, as this adds an extra level of motivation. Regularly checking in with yourself on progress made towards all goals will help ensure that skill development remains focused.

Additionally, this self-evaluation will ensure that you make necessary changes due to market conditions or personal life events. Finding a mentor who has been through the same journey can provide invaluable guidance on setting goals and overcoming obstacles along the way. As your career advances, remember to take time to celebrate successes while keeping focus on continuing objectives throughout the journey ahead!

4

Important Do's and Don'ts for The Sandbox

Don't be Your Assistant or the Lunch Girl

PLAYGROUND RULE #4

Stand Out for the Right Reasons

When you are around men or clients, don't accept tasks that are the responsibility of a less senior staff member, or administrative assistant (such as making copies, getting coffee, or retrieving lunch for the group). If you are asked to "go fetch," be kind and advise that you will have a more appropriate person handle such a task. Then, ask your assistant to enter the room, introduce him or her, and make that person available for such requests. If you don't have an administrative assistant, solicit the assistance of another appropriate person, such as the receptionist, a clerk in the mail room, or another staff member. In the worst-case scenario, if no other person is available, ask that such tasks be rotated or coordinated so they can be taken care of before the meeting (pre-ordering lunch or having coffee available).

If during a meeting, you, as the only female, are repeatedly asked to take notes of the meeting, step out to "fetch" amenities for the group, or make copies, suggest that members of the team rotate completing these tasks to include the men in the room. Remind your superior that you are missing important parts of the meeting by leaving the room. Be direct about your position, typical responsibilities, and work priorities. Set clear boundaries. You may not be able to avoid these tasks 100% of the time, but you will learn when to help out and when to push back. Open and honest communication is always best, such as: "If you don't mind, I will need to ask my supervisor, John, if I can take time away from our urgent project to make copies. It might be better to ask an appropriate staff person. I am happy to coordinate the copies for you if you wish. Maybe your assistant can handle this task?"

If you believe you are being asked to complete tasks more appropriate for an administrative assistant because you are the only female in the room, gently remind your superior that his request might amount to gender discrimination. If possible, use a little humor. If he ignores your objection, address the issue with a superior who has influence over the violator, or, worst case, take your concern to HR.

Being the "yes" or "fetch" girl might be appealing in demonstrating how you are a "team player;" however, it is not going to make you more popular or foster your career. Being asked to do these unsuitable tasks is disrespectful and discriminatory, especially if you are the only female or person asked. You are losing valuable information and contribution time during your absence, which can ultimately harm your career. "How many successful men in the workplace do you see picking up their boss's lunch or coffee? ... Sure, maybe there are special exceptions when your boss is in fire drill mode or decides to treat a group for getting his coffee—but don't make it a regular thing. And if your male peers aren't chipping in, you shouldn't be doing it, either."[1]

Organizing Non-Work Matters

Don't fall into the trap of becoming the "mom at work" by undertaking tasks for your team that take you away from important work, meetings, or networking events, such as organizing team-wide lunches, bonding activities or parties. While your efforts may be appreciated, they will only do a little to establish you as an influential leader. The same is true for client-related and marketing events. Limit your participation in overseeing planning and providing input. Instead, focus on work-related matters to help you progress within the company. Your work responsibilities are far more valuable than running errands for others. Instead, strive to contribute meaningfully to projects and initiatives that will further develop your career!

Pick Your Battles—Sharing a Controversial Opinion

Be gracious with your opinions and tolerant of others. Do not patronize people or act like a "know-it-all." Be respectful, and don't shut down a discussion partner just because you disagree with them. Implying a superior is stupid or does not know what they are discussing will not impress or further your career. Show interest in others' opinions and ask them to explain their thoughts and ideas. You might just learn something.

More importantly, especially when working with a superior or a client, learn how to add value by contributing positively to the discussion. Try to disagree without being disagreeable. Repeat the other person's suggestion ("If I understand you correctly, you are suggesting....") and then offer your proposed improvements over existing suggestions in a gentle and non-degrading way. Acknowledging and clarifying your superior's argument makes you appear less aggressive in challenging their opinion.

My father, who climbed the German Air Force and NATO ranks post-WWII, frequently discussed "how not to alienate a superior" with me. [NATO is "The North Atlantic Treaty Organization," an intergovernmental military alliance between 30 member states—28 European and two North American]. He believed that avoiding aggressive opposition to challenging opinions or questionable orders was critical. Opposition might appear disrespectful, and defying a direct order could ruin a career. Instead, if he disagreed, he would engage in gentle discussion to redirect his superior to my father's viewpoint and subtly manipulate his superiors into thinking it was their idea. This strategy, he emphasized, is sound when dealing with superiors or opposing parties.

Both JR and I learned this technique, which allowed us to resolve concerns and complex issues between our clients and their deal partners across the table, ultimately helping to close transactions successfully. Understanding each party's specific situation, needs, and concerns is critical to offering alternative suggestions and compromises. Deal goals can be achieved if these issues can be communicated in a non-controversial and gentle manner.

Knowledge is Power in Negotiations

When entering a complex negotiation or antagonistic situation, prepare to defend your position with proper backup arguments and information and ensure that you have the opportunity to share your thoughts. If needed, stand up to be noticed: "I would like to share some pertinent information on this topic that might help resolve this issue. May I speak?" If your team is looking for more information on a new or challenging topic, make yourself known to be the person with a precise understanding of the subject matter and offer to educate them with a short presentation. This way, you are educating your coworkers on a topic of interest while simultaneously strengthening your credibility and their impressions of you. If you are participating in a meeting where you have been asked to report on a matter or a topic of interest, do your very best to be prepared and anticipate the questions that might be asked. Remember, knowledge is power. I can't emphasize this enough. Take the time to thoroughly research any issues that might be raised and resource any pointers from other colleagues or superiors who can help suggest the best way to prepare. Adding value to others with your contributions is very important. By helpfully contributing, your superiors or clients will not ignore you when you raise your hand or stand up to speak in subsequent times.

Being a Whistleblower

A whistleblower is an individual who courageously reports illegal, unethical, or dishonest activities within the workplace. These individuals play a vital role in detecting and preventing such activities, which helps to uphold public trust and promote a healthy work environment. To encourage the reporting of wrongful activities within an organization, employers should establish a secure reporting procedure that ensures the safety of employees from any backlash and allows them to be taken seriously. Retaliation against whistleblowers is illegal and can take various forms, including termination, demotion, defamation, harassment, or any other adverse action. Fortunately, whistleblowers are protected by several laws, such as the Whistleblower Protection Act and the Sarbanes-Oxley Act [2]. Unfortunately, as a whistleblower, if you need to pursue legal action, it likely means you have already experienced retaliation at the expense of your job.

If you are asked to do something controversial, unethical, or illegal, protect yourself from potential liabilities by taking detailed notes on the matter and the person making the request. Seek advice and support from a trusted superior or colleague to intervene and resolve the issue in your favor. Then, extricate yourself from the situation. Remember that dealing with bad behavior lies with management and superiors, and blowing the whistle could potentially harm your career. Seek support and protection from important allies before taking any drastic action to help preserve your job.

Monitor Your Emotions

It's important to note that controlling emotions is not gender-specific; both genders can benefit from emotional regulation in the workplace. That being said, here are some examples of how women can control their emotions in a professional setting:

If you find a situation is making you angry or upset, or you are about to get emotional, excuse yourself and re-group. This situation has happened to all of us. You do not want to lose control and give another person the satisfaction of having upset you. That person will find a way to use your reaction to their advantage and portray you as whiny or weak—especially if you are a woman. It's acceptable to say, "Excuse me, I will be right back." If you do happen to cry, don't fret. Be honest and say, "I didn't mean to get emotional. I have had a tough day, and this topic is upsetting. Let me re-group, and we can talk later." You will appear stronger and more in control if you own up to your emotions; failing to do so may give others a reason not to take you seriously.

Taking a few deep breaths can help you calm down and refocus in moments of stress. When communicating with colleagues or superiors, try to keep emotions in check and express yourself in an assertive but professional tone. Make a conscious effort to reframe negative self-talk into positive self-talk. Focus on your strengths and accomplishments, and avoid negative self-talk or self-doubt that can lead to negative emotions. Be bold and talk to a trusted colleague or mentor if you're struggling to control your emotions in certain workplace situations or with certain colleagues. They may have helpful insights or be able to provide support and guidance.

Avoid Being Too Easily Offended— Difficult Personalities

Work environments can be stressful, and there may be times where you are not treated with the respect and dignity you deserve. Take an occasional curt tone of voice or dismissive response with a grain of salt. Assess the situation, and if you find that your violator is experiencing high stress, give them a break. Address the behavior later when matters have calmed down: "Hope things are better today than they were yesterday. I could tell you were very stressed when we communicated. Please let me know next time if there is anything I can do to help make things easier." More often than not, that person will realize they behaved badly and apologize. However, if you find you are a constant target of the violator, address the issue with a superior or, worst case, review your concerns with HR. If you are dealing regularly with difficult personalities, keep reading for my recommendations in Chapter 9 later in this book.

Male Banter—The Boys' Club

Take a deep breath and handle the challenges of being around guys with grace—mainly for your sanity. The boys' club is inevitable if you work in a male-dominated environment, and although making headway into such a club may improve your career, to do so, you will have to tolerate some inappropriate stories and banter.

However, there *is* a line, and "staying cool" doesn't mean letting the guys cross it—sexual harassment, discrimination, or any other kind of abuse is NEVER okay. Don't compromise who you are to "fit in." The key is to become part of your male colleagues' 'circle of trust' by allowing them to be themselves *up to a point* without running to HR to complain about bad behavior. More on this later in Chapter 9.

Be Confident, Not Difficult

Don't act like a "tough girl," and don't act aggressively to others like you have an ax to grind. Don't use foul language, and don't demean or discredit others. It won't earn you respect and will be viewed with suspicion. Be confident. Take advantage of your own strengths and best qualities. My mother said it best: "You don't have to act like a man. You have the one weapon men don't have. You are a woman. Something a man can't help but pay attention to and something they need to survive. It is a gentle but powerful weapon. Use your qualities to your advantage." Be direct, assertive, and specific—with a kind but firm tone of voice. If you have to raise your voice to be heard occasionally, go for it. My mom was beautiful and tough, and she enjoyed working with men. She commanded respect by rarely letting bad behavior slide without taking notice and responding in a manner to educate. I took her cue.

At my job, if the men in the room tried to interrupt me or speak over or for me disrespectfully, I would stand, raise my hand, and raise my voice. "Okay, gents, it is my turn now. Please listen!" Sometimes, I would have to bang on the table or simply stay standing until they realized I would not sit down until I was heard. I would keep a steady but firm voice and add humor if needed. JR similarly handles her male colleagues. She is a force of nature, and her voice and mannerisms resonate to command respect. You know when JR is in the room.

You do not have to use foul language or be disrespectful or nasty to get to the top.

We all recognize that women are often reluctant to play hardball and raise their voices in meetings as they might be perceived as "combative," "emotional," "difficult," or "bitchy." However, I agree with one of my favorite journals. You should take the step to be heard (when appropriate) and be "hard," "difficult," or "aggressive." And don't apologize for it. Own it.[3]

If you are ignored or interrupted rudely or disrespectfully by your male colleagues, don't be offended; however, you should not let them shut you down, either. Learn how to create boundaries to foster respect and trust. Express concerns in a non-threatening manner to avoid putting the other person on the defensive. Don't be accusatory or put on a "bitchy behavior." If you put men on the defensive or embarrass them in front of their colleagues, they will stop listening to you or may write you off as a person not to trust.

Worse, they may go out of their way to sabotage your person or career.

Please share your opinions or concerns gently, with a bit of humor, and set them straight. Use the moment to educate and help them understand why their statements are problematic. Stand up if needed and make yourself heard. Insist on communicating for a better understanding. "I have something to say on this. Please listen." Whatever you do, be prepared, and don't give them a reason to challenge your contributions. Prove them wrong! If you show them a better way, they will not talk over you or ignore you next time.

Be Statuesque rather than Sexy

How you present yourself physically can reflect on the quality of your work. Appearing professional and dressing appropriately for the workplace makes an impression on those around you, ultimately improving your position within the company or organization. Keep in mind that people may judge others by their physical appearance, so it is essential to look neat and tidy at all times.

Foremost, don't be a distraction. You want people to focus on you and not how you look. Study your company's dress code and culture, making a conscious effort to present yourself professionally. "Many businesses still see what employees wear as an important indicator of their brand, and it also affects employees' perceptions individually."[4] "...how clothing deemed to be "unsuitable" by colleagues or customers can result in women being viewed as less competent or of lower status than men in the same working environment." Id. It does not matter that many companies have relaxed their dress code requirements in response to the Covid pandemic. "...women still remain more at risk for negative assumptions based on their attire, when compared to men." Id.

Plain and elegant is better than sexy tight clothes with cleavage and loud perfume. Aim for grace, dignity, and modesty. You want to be seen as an elegant contributor, not a distraction or controversial conversation starter based on your clothing choices. My mother always told me that how you dress and maintain your hair, nails, and toes, is a reflection of who you are as a person. This includes the heels of your shoes. Mom's pet peeve: Make sure your shoes are capped! She would say: "There is nothing worse than walking behind a well-dressed woman and her shoes have scraped and uncapped heels with exposed shoe nails clanking on the pavement!" It would make her crazy!

Ask for help at your favorite stores if you are not sure how to dress your best or take a friend you admire to shop for clothes. Ask a makeup artist to help you look neat and elegant. Find a good hairdresser to give you the latest styles best suited to you. You don't have to spend a fortune. Expensive name brands won't necessarily make you look any better.

Take out five minutes at the end of each day to select your outfit for the next day. This way, you are not rushing around to get ready in the morning. If you look messy, you will give the impression that your office, your work and your contributions are lacking in quality. I firmly believe that a polished appearance can boost your confidence and positively impact how you approach your responsibilities at work and home. This can result in garnering the respect and recognition you deserve.

"A 2016 study found a correlation between women dressing well and being paid better at work. A survey by PayScale found the same as well for both men and women, with those who dress in business attire making nearly $20,000 more in salary than those who wear uniforms."[5]

"Another study found people who put on business attire, like a suit or skirt and blouse, processed information differently as they felt the power to link abstract concepts more easily."[6] "So dressing smart makes you feel smart." Id. "Wear what makes you feel comfortable, confident, and professional…but know that you're sending strong signals with your clothing, so make sure they're the signals you want to send."[7]

Don't Date a Colleague or Superior

We all know couples who met at work and have successful long-term relationships. This seems inevitable if you spend most of your waking hours at work with folks with common interests.

However, relationships at work are problematic and can put both parties in a difficult position, especially if the male is a superior. If the relationship begins as an affair, how would that ultimately impact the career of the female? Who would have to leave the job if the company had an anti-dating or anti-nepotism policy? If you date a colleague, whether or not there is such a policy, matters become complicated if you break up. Why put yourself through the drama of possibly being fired for violating company policy or, after a breakup, suffering through the aftermath where both of you work? It will negatively impact you and the colleagues and staff you work with.

My best recommendation is don't do it. The risks are far too great.

Take the time to evaluate your situation and understand how much you care about your job. "One in three romantic office relationships will end in at least one person being fired, according to a survey of 150 HR executives conducted by hiring firm Challenger, Gray, and Christmas. Things aren't necessarily better for those who don't get fired. The survey found that 17 percent of employers chose to move at least one employee to a different department, and five percent of these affairs led to litigation."[8]

Yet, despite the risks, recent statistics advise that more than half of employees have engaged in a romantic relationship with a colleague.[9]

If you believe you have found your soulmate, please keep the following tips in mind: First, research your company's policies on dating and reporting requirements to your HR department. If there are strict policies, you should follow them, especially if you are in a relationship with a subordinate or superior. Statistics indicate that 41% of employees are not aware of company policies on workplace romance.[10]

Maintaining a secret relationship is complex and might ultimately risk both of your careers. Secondly, before you start dating, have open and candid conversations regarding your expectations and potential consequences to your career, including after a breakup. Ask yourselves: will dating this person affect your professional goals, reputation, and contributions to your company? According to a recent survey, "34% [of colleagues] believe that relationships between coworkers at different levels are unacceptable."[11] Take a hard look at your company's culture. How will you be perceived? Dating a colleague might raise eyebrows with your other team members. As a superior, whose interests will you put first, the teams' or yours? Your professionalism may be called into question. What if you break up? Will the other person hold a grudge and potentially ruin your career? What would it be like to work with an ex day-to-day? Will you be able to work together and remain professional and civil without bad feelings affecting the morale of those around you? Third, don't use company property, funds, or technology to boost your relationship or express your feelings—and don't conduct your office romance at the office (especially at office parties where alcohol is flowing). Keep your relationship private and off of social media. If your relationship is work-related, you may find you have nothing outside of work in common, and your relationship may fizzle quickly.

In summary, avoid dating a superior or subordinate. Many companies today prohibit such relationships. Your colleagues may interpret any promotions, raises, and higher profile work assignments in favor of your "honey," regardless of whether they are well deserved, as "preferential treatment." Your company might view such actions as negative—a conflict of interest in violation of company policy, putting the subordinate's and the superior's job on the line. The CEO of McDonald's lost his job in 2019 for dating a subordinate. The company cited, "It is not appropriate to show favoritism or make business decisions based on emotions or friendships rather than on the best interests of the Company."[12]

Regardless of the actual terms of the company's policy, the concern is the risk of potential problems that might arise if the relationship ends badly. These problems include harassment, retaliation, and legal liability to the company. As the #MeToo movement has emphasized, where there is a power imbalance, the executive's perception of what constitutes consent may not be shared by the subordinate. News involving Matt Lauer, Placido Domingo, Bill Cosby, Harvey Weinstein, Steve Wynn, Leslie Moonves, and Charlie Walk are prime examples.[13,14]

Finally, if the company's leadership determines trouble is brewing and there is a risk of a sexual harassment suit if the relationship turns sour, who do you think is likely to be blamed and lose their job? "Even today, a boss-subordinate relationship is viewed as strategic on the woman's part," says Rebecca Chory, Ph.D., who studies workplace interactions at Maryland's Frostburg State University. Yes, there may be exceptions (McDonald's CEO); however, they are few and far between.[15]

You Don't Have to Be a Sports Fan to Be Interesting

You are not required to be a sports fan to succeed in a male-dominated work environment. However, if you are interested in becoming more educated on the top stories of your sports audience, download an app to help you stay updated, such as Bleacher Report or ESPN. I get flash reports on my iWatch and enjoy being the first to educate my male friends on top news.

If sports are not your thing, find a hobby or extracurricular activity worth sharing. At work and in my friend groups, we had very diverse interests ranging from those who enjoyed boating and fishing, hiking and diving, running and gym workouts, healthy living, museums and the arts, world travel, learning languages, shopping, volunteering for local causes and charities, current news, history buffs, TV show and movie junkies, cooking and wine, latest electronics and gadgets, and book lovers. Conversations were always exciting, and we quickly knew who to go to for expert advice on a topic or interest. Make time to find a hobby or special interest and educate yourself. Then, share with others to make yourself known as the person with the most knowledge on the subject. Generally, keep up with current events but avoid aggressive political arguments, especially with superiors and clients. If you must engage, understand both sides of the argument and listen patiently. Be gentle with your opinions if you share them, and gracefully acknowledge other viewpoints. Nothing good ever comes from heated political discussions or treating others like you are a 'know-it-all' and everyone else is stupid. You will quickly alienate important relationships, both personal and at work.

You Don't Have to Work All Night to be respected

In our day as young lawyers, we were expected to work hard and very late hours, often working all night long to complete a project timely under unrealistic deadlines. A lot has stayed the same today for associates in similar industries. Despite your work demands, you must find a way to care for yourself. You will only function at your best with sleep, food, and a healthy lifestyle. Drinking caffeine, a Red Bull, or other high-energy drink on the hour is not the solution and may put your health at risk. If your work demands are overwhelming, talk to your boss. If you are uncomfortable doing so, consult another superior colleague with influence or HR to help negotiate a more regular work schedule or intermittent days off to help you recover and recharge in a healthy manner.

Don't Be That Girl—Slut or Drunk

For women in the workforce, drawing a firm line of respect for how they are treated is critical. Fueling the rumor mill by sleeping with superiors or colleagues will not give you any advantages in the long term, if at all. As we noted earlier, these relationships are risky and likely to get you fired, especially if they run afoul of company policy. You will also lose the respect of your colleagues and become part of a negative conversation, likely to harm your career. The same applies to drinking. Know your limits, and don't try to keep up with the boys. You don't want to be unable to control the outcome. Being "that girl" will not earn you a "plus" in the reputation column.

5

Building Relationships for Long Term Success

Get to Know Your Team Leaders and Management

Literal facetime with your colleagues is important. Get to know the members and leaders of your team. Don't be afraid to report on your work, regularly highlight your accomplishments, talk through questions you may have as they arise (after exhausting appropriate research yourself), and seek feedback when projects are concluded. Complete your projects by making strong contributions that showcase your value to the team. A work product that makes a good impression will foster the trust and support you need to progress within your career, especially from your immediate superiors.

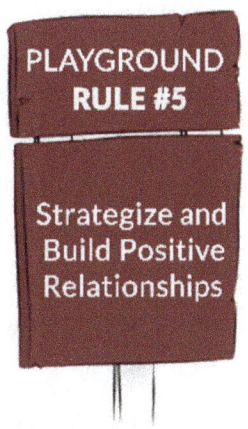

PLAYGROUND RULE #5

Strategize and Build Positive Relationships

Be a Team Player; Build Relationships

You gain respect by building good relationships with your male and female colleagues, whether they are subordinate or superior in rank. Pay

83

particular notice to your peers and superiors who directly or indirectly influence how you achieve your goals and job duties. Be respectful to subordinates and staff members who are critical for completing important job support functions, such as your administrative assistants, associates, runners, and those working in the copy room and after-hours typing center. You cannot get to the goal line without them. Additionally, having strong internal relationships gives you a better chance of receiving assistance and furthers your career goals. Be careful to draw a line of professionalism with the staff, your peers, and superiors. This will help you maintain relationships that are built on mutual respect.

Learn from Role Models

Start by identifying individuals within your workplace who excel in areas you are interested in or want to improve. Observe their daily routines, habits, and interpersonal skills, noting qualities and behaviors you would like to emulate. Actively seeking feedback and advice from role models and implementing their insights can foster growth and development in your work. Evaluating your progress and refining your approach based on their feedback can lead to continued learning. The positive commentary from well-respected role models can also serve as valuable support and validation.

Seek Suitable Mentors—Inside or Outside of the Office

A mentor is someone with senior career experience who can answer questions, offer advice, foster confidence, and help you navigate the obstacles of your work environment. A mentor gives relevant advice that promotes growth within your career, area of work, and company, making you better at your job and improving your performance. They understand the work culture and the people of influence and inspire you to use your talents to benefit the company and yourself. You can find mentors inside or outside of your workplace.

If your company has a mentoring program, you should seek male and female mentors to gain diverse perspectives. It's best to choose a senior role model who has already achieved success, as they can offer invaluable advice and support. Mentors can also provide feedback on work assignments, help you communicate with difficult superiors, and help you pursue promotions.

When approaching a potential mentor, express your respect for their input and explain how their mentorship can help you grow. If you are looking for feedback on work assignments, ensure that they are completed to the best of your ability to impress them and encourage their support. Your mentor will only be interested in helping you if you provide your best work. It would help if you also considered joining groups within the company or organizations outside of work that support mentoring, such as women's groups of professionals in similar or complementary fields of work, as they can provide additional opportunities for career growth. "Having a mentor, especially a female mentor from the same industry, is a wonderful way to build skills and knowledge. Suppose they're holding a position of power and respect, even better. In that case, their reputation can help bolster the reputation of those they mentor, lending authority to the mentee as they build their own profile within the business."[1]

External mentors can be just as valuable as internal ones, providing fresh perspectives and insights from different industries, fields, or career paths. Selecting mentors with diverse backgrounds and points of view broadens your perspective, leading to new ideas and concepts that can benefit your career growth. If you need help finding a mentor, ask for referrals from friends, family, and colleagues. Additionally, you can use certain networking platforms to connect with potential mentors. For example, you can start by contacting senior colleagues within your company or attending networking events and conferences within your industry to meet potential mentors.

Also, outside associations and organizations, including women's groups and local charities, often have mentorship programs that can help you connect with experienced professionals in your industry. Don't be afraid to reach out and ask for guidance—many professionals are willing to help mentor younger employees. As you look for mentors, try to identify people you relate to in some way, such as sharing a place of birth, alma mater, work industry, hobby, or other mutual connection. Once you've identified a potential mentor, think about the areas of your career where the mentor can be most helpful. Do you need help with certain business concepts, work issues, mastering certain skills, business strategies, dealing with difficult work personalities, office politics, or career progression? [2] Be specific about why you need their guidance, whether it's industry-specific or work-style advice, and be clear about how the mentor can help with your goals. To maximize the mentor's time, outline your goals before the meeting, limit the meeting to a reasonable period, and make it convenient for them to attend (such as over coffee or lunch).

Maintain contact with your mentors as you advance in your career. Be open to new mentors as circumstances evolve, such as changing jobs or starting a family. Keep them abreast of how you've used their guidance and related successes, sharing insights that may benefit them. Please return the favor, and don't forget to thank them with a personal note or small gift. Nurturing these relationships is vital; view your mentors as your personal board of directors, as they may prove valuable as referral or recommendation sources.[3]

After benefiting from a mentor's guidance, consider paying it forward by becoming a mentor yourself. Please share your experience and knowledge with the next generation of professionals to help them succeed in your field. Through mentoring, you can significantly impact future generations and contribute to a more diverse and inclusive workforce—valuable contributions your company will notice. You will have fostered important leadership skills for your career and personal growth.

Find a Sponsor or Advocate within Your Company

The difference between mentors and sponsors is that mentors talk *with* you and give you advice. In contrast, sponsors talk *about* you and give you opportunities. Sponsors essentially act as your champion—and actively seek ways to promote your career and skill development.

Sponsors use their connections to advocate and cheerlead for a less experienced employee, actively participating in their career growth. They will be the ones to highlight your abilities when opportunities arise, they will speak up for you, and they will introduce you to people who can advance your career.[4]

It's advantageous to have both a mentor and a sponsor; however, as highlighted earlier, sponsors play an active role in your promotion. Behind closed doors, they will communicate your accomplishments and talents, helping promote your qualifications for advancement.

You will want to attract an influential, well-respected sponsor known for promoting talented employees. Do your research and find out who they are at your company. Once you identify a potential sponsor, figure out how to become an employee they would love to support and promote. Volunteer to work on projects with the sponsor to showcase your talents and make every effort to perform your best and exceed expectations. Use these work opportunities to communicate your accomplishments, successes, and values and to showcase your leadership skills. Practice your elevator speech. More on how to develop one later in Chapter 6. When your sponsor has knowledge and personal experience with your successes and abilities, it will be easier for him or her to sell your talents. Know your career goals and share them with your sponsor. Your sponsor can then match your goals to opportunities that arise.

Focus on colleagues who believe in you and openly endorse you within the organization (including customers and clients). They'll be your strongest allies and top supporters.

Most importantly, remember that sponsorship is earned. Sponsors must be convinced of your abilities. If sponsors believe in you, they will be your best advocates.

Recruit Allies: How Men Can Help

To establish allies within the workplace, don't hesitate to search for men open to supporting female employees in male-dominated fields. These men can be identified by their thoughtfulness in listening to women's thoughts, endorsing their ideas in meetings, challenging gender bias, and actively praising female colleagues in the presence of others.[5]

If these male allies see you in an uncomfortable position with a violator, they will step in to admonish the bad behavior, extract you from the situation, or offer to be a witness for you with HR.

As you make male friends at work, turn them into allies. Educate them on how they can help support you and their other female colleagues. To help educate them, please give them a copy of this book and our first book *Play Nice!*

Breaking Into the 'Boys' Club':

> Meaning of the Boys' Club

In a survey of 1,500 working women, InHerSight found that 54.1 percent say they have worked at a company with a "boys' club" culture. A boys' club culture is run and dominated by men to the detriment, exclusion, or abuse of women and minorities.[6] They are often informal social networks of men who promote the company from within, providing networking, professional mentoring, and work opportunities exclusively to boys' club members. "And since so many [boys' clubs] are also havens for toxicity, relying on a degree of sexist humor and objectification for their camaraderie, women are rarely admitted."[7]

➤ The Dilemma of Tolerating Bad Behavior

For example, let's say you're in an all-male staff meeting, and the men keep commenting on a female administrative assistant's body parts each time she comes into the room, rating her on a 1-10 scale, and then laughing about each other's comments. The banter makes you uncomfortable, but you say nothing for fear of backlash. Being the only woman in the room can be intimidating. There will be upsetting situations where you wish you would have called out your male colleagues, said something, or done something differently, but you didn't. Tolerating the bad behavior or remaining silent can pose a wrong signal about your approval of their comments, and the men are likely to continue misbehaving.

However, if you decide to speak up, what you say and how you say it might make a difference in your future relationship with your male coworkers and your career. Let's say the men are not happy with your tone of voice or what you say; they may decide to exclude you from their group meetings, social interactions, or work opportunities-effectively deciding you will not be part of their boys' club.

➤ Using the 'Boys Club' to Your Advantage

Trying to build a relationship with the boys' club can bolster your professional growth if you find yourself among the few women in your office or industry. This exclusive network is where deals are made, the best strategies are shared, plans are devised, and problems are tackled. As a woman, you can gain valuable insights into how your male colleagues think, strategize, and solve problems. If your male peers respect and appreciate your contributions, they may support and welcome you into their professional realm. While seeking approval and inclusion from the boys' club may not be easy, it can be a necessary step towards establishing yourself in the industry. An unmatched feeling of recognition and admiration comes with being acknowledged and valued for your skills and talents, especially among your male colleagues.

To fit into the boys' club, you need to establish trust with your male colleagues. However, this does not mean compromising your beliefs, tolerating inappropriate behavior, or participating in conversations that make you uncomfortable. Instead, establish clear boundaries that represent your values. Additionally, it would help if you worked hard to showcase your intellect and capabilities to get their attention. Doing this will require more effort than your male peers looking for similar recognition.

If you encounter inappropriate male banter—and you will, you have several response options. First, you could listen, take notes, and turn them in to HR. However, this risks exclusion from their group or possible retaliation if they find out you complained to HR. Second, you could be confrontational and say with a raised or stern voice: "Come on, gentlemen. Please stop talking about her like that. You are making me uncomfortable! If you continue your behavior, I will turn you into HR!" Many experts believe this is the best way to combat bad behavior since it catches the perpetrator off guard and challenges his manhood and prestige, especially if you admonish him in front of an audience. However, this approach will likely put the violator on the defensive, and you may have created an enemy for challenging his manhood.

We agree certain situations require confrontation, especially if you are encountering repetitive sexual harassment, bullying, or other demeaning behavior. However, you will likely receive a defensive response, potentially risking exclusion from the boys' club or some other form of retaliation.

Instead of outright accusatory confrontation, consider a gentler but firm approach that gets their attention but leaves their ego intact, especially if the perpetrator is among a group. The goal is to communicate that they've misbehaved and are being offered an opportunity to fix the behavior going forward, positively, without any repercussions. They may appreciate that you are trying to help and keep them out of trouble, fostering trust with your gentle approach. For example, stand up (to get their attention), smile, and say with a firm but gentle voice, "Now, now, gentlemen. Simmer down. You are being inappropriate. (You could add: "If she were your sister or daughter, you would not want guys making those comments about her, would you?" Or, you could add: "What would your mom say if she heard your comments?") "Let's be respectful to your female colleagues going forward."

Another approach is to note that you care about your male colleagues and don't want them to get into trouble. You could add: "If someone hears you, you could be subject to sexual harassment or gender discrimination claims! Let's talk more about respect and boundaries!"

Establish a clear boundary of self-respect each time you encounter inappropriate behavior. If it persists, reiterate your previous warning and assert that you prioritize their best interests. Among my male friends, I can raise two fingers (after an inappropriate comment is made) as a reminder of a prior reprimand, and they all know now what I will say. In many cases, they will cut me off and immediately apologize. Use an applicable playground rule from *Play Nice* to help communicate the inappropriate behavior: "Respect the playground and its players!" or "Treat players how you want to be treated!" or "Treat your colleagues how you would want your wife, sister, daughter or mother to be treated!" In a recent article, Audrey Nelson said it well: *"The good ol' boys club needs to know when it crosses the line. Set boundaries and address issues from a position of strength, not weakness. Don't say what they did wrong (whining and negative); say what you want them to do (positive)."*[8]

In this context, another playground rule from *Play Nice* will be helpful for you regarding the treatment of colleagues: "Use nice words, be polite, and have good manners."

How you handle sexual harassment will depend on the nature of the harassment and the personality type of the abuser. Responding to a superior who is conditioning your job on a physical relationship with him is much more severe than taming a group of male colleagues who are commenting on a female colleague's body parts in your presence.

For more on this topic, please see *Play Nice*. Using a little humor in certain circumstances, especially when dealing with a group of violators, will likely diffuse a defensive response to your caution about the behavior. When you offer positive feedback on how to behave better, you are more likely to be viewed as looking out for the perpetrators, which might foster trust and is less likely to create enemies at work.

➤ How to Break into the Boys' Club

Breaking into the boys' club can be challenging, but it is possible with persistence and a strategic approach. Here are some general suggestions:

Seek out male colleagues and managers for professional relationships. Attend networking events, schedule one-on-one meetings, and engage in social activities to break the ice and create rapport. Strive for excellence in your work and areas of subject matter expertise. Make yourself heard when opportunities arise to demonstrate how your expert knowledge adds value for the benefit of your company.

Don't let fear or self-doubt keep you from sharing your ideas and perspectives. Use confident and assertive communication styles to ensure your voice is heard. Persist when advocating for your professional growth or challenging exclusionary practices. Set goals and hold yourself accountable for meeting them. Don't let anyone else define your success or worth in the workplace.

Most importantly, take a deep breath and handle the challenges of being around guys with grace. The boys' club is inevitable if you work in a male-dominated environment.

These tips can empower you to navigate the boys' club and advance your career. While it may involve tolerating certain inappropriate stories and banter from your male counterparts, it's crucial to set boundaries and not allow disrespectful behavior to go unchecked. As noted early in this book, there *is* a line, and "staying cool" doesn't mean letting the guys cross it—sexual harassment, discrimination, or any other kind of abuse is NEVER okay. Don't compromise who you are to "fit in." The key is to become part of your male colleagues' 'circle of trust' by allowing them to be themselves *up to a point* without running to HR to complain about bad behaviors.

Up to a point means alerting your male colleagues with a bit of humor when they have crossed the line, or their comments might get them into trouble with others. JR and I learned to laugh aloud and direct their attention to something they said: "OMG, did you hear what you just said? What if someone said that about your daughter or wife? Surely that would not be acceptable!" Use your objections as teaching moments. Your male colleagues will appreciate you looking out for them.

Whether we like it or not, learning from your male colleagues can further your career, especially over a beer or in other social settings. It is important to avoid alienating men as potential allies, sponsors, and mentors. "The secret to successfully maneuvering these scenarios is to be yourself and emphasize your professionalism, the value you add, and your ability to handle the guys with grace, aplomb [self-confidence], and a little bit of humor." [9]

Create Your Own Girls' Club or Women's Mentoring Network

Regardless of whether you choose to break into the boys' club, take the initiative to create your own girls' club or women's mentoring network. Women deserve mentorship, sponsorship, and opportunities just as much as their male counterparts. Seek support from your senior colleagues and recruit equally motivated members to learn from the women who have forged a path to success at your organization. Recruit female mentors and colleagues who have successfully navigated male-dominated workplaces to participate. Establishing relationships with your female colleagues is an excellent idea for your career and important for your health and well-being. Take advantage, even if leadership at your organization is initially not supportive.

Establish yourself as a leader at your organization by creating a women's program and promoting its value and benefits to the company, namely increased retention and recruitment of talented women for greater innovation, diversity, and creative thought. Seek support from your senior management and HR, and invite men who are your allies and supportive of your initiatives. Their participation and engagement will encourage other men to join and promote your efforts. When a boys' culture dominates your organization, hiring more women at senior levels is good to help promote diversity and foster more equal representation. As we will cover later in this book, a more diverse workforce ultimately translates to a more profitable company.

➢ Create Your Board of Directors Outside of Work

Develop a supportive network of trusted advisors beyond your professional circle, also known as a 'Board of Directors,' for your personal growth. Identify individuals who genuinely have your best interests at heart, are not in any way competing with you, and are devoid of professional envy. Consult with these individuals whenever you seek genuine feedback and counsel. Their insights can play a crucial role in accelerating your career growth and aiding you in overcoming challenging circumstances. That being said, solely relying on your Board of Directors to promote your career growth is not wise. Ultimately, it is up to you to take the necessary steps to advance your career.

➤ Building a Network of Women Outside of the Office

Join women's groups or professional organizations in your industry to build and expand your support network. Participating and contributing to such groups will help foster opportunities for mentorship, knowledge exchange, skills training, cross-promotion, and marketing your work expertise for client development purposes. Join fundraising and volunteer opportunities for local charities to get acquainted with professional men and women from various industries, similar to how JR and I crossed paths. Through these groups and occasions, we were fortunate to meet some incredible people who became valuable connections and referrals for business, clients, and friends.

6

The Importance of Marketing Skills

The Importance of Learning Marketing Skills

As my career progressed, I recognized the value of observing and imitating co-workers skilled in marketing at business meals, industry conferences, and social events. I helped resource client prospects and worked on marketing strategies to sell our firm's talents. I developed detailed work proposals outlining why the prospect should hire our law firm instead of the competition. Understanding the needs and preferences of your target client is vital to creating a successful marketing proposal with goals, strategies, a budget, and metrics for success. I advise that you join a client development/marketing group, and if none exists at your company, start your own and invite others to collaborate. Work with your colleagues to develop compelling content for your marketing proposals. Strategize industry networking opportunities for client prospects and optimize your work website to attract new business. If available, draw upon your company's marketing department whenever you need assistance with your elevator pitch, client prospect identification, or marketing strategy for new work. They can help you with market research, branding, advertising, and social media marketing. Since each target client is unique, adjust your approach to accommodate their specific needs and preferences. Remember that your company's marketing department is an essential resource to utilize. Honing in on these skills will help you break through the glass ceiling and even out the playing field between you and your male counterparts.

Understand the importance of networking and building relationships with influential men and women in your company and industry. I found breaking into the boys' club particularly helpful. It taught me how to communicate more effectively with male colleagues and clients, including understanding their communication styles and adjusting my communications accordingly. I gained insights into the male perspective on marketing campaigns and strategies while additionally developing competence in traditionally male-dominated skills, such as negotiating and assertiveness. Building relationships with male colleagues also helped me learn to navigate office politics and power dynamics, increasing my influence and impact within my law firms.

Build-Out Your Network of Contacts

As you commence your career journey, build out your network of existing and potential contacts using any address lists you may have created over the years, whether for holiday cards, parties you may have organized, events you worked on in high school or college, for charity or fundraising, or any other activities, including with family, friends, classmates at college or university, parent acquaintances, and any prior job connections. Categorize your list to identify potential resources for new business, referral resources for new work, and mentors who might help you sharpen your marketing tools. Schedule regular periods each week when you focus solely on ways to expand your network of potential customers or clients and go to work. Identify your target and open communications. Send them a personal note or email on a topic of interest, schedule a lunch, or coordinate to meet for happy hour or at a social event. Don't be afraid to let them know you have a new job and would like to explore opportunities to work together. Highlight how you and your company can add value to help them achieve success.

Develop Your Elevator Speech and Brand

There are things you need to learn early in your career. Such as how to respond to a request for an introduction in 30 seconds or less—just long enough for an elevator ride—your "elevator speech." Your elevator speech should contain:

- ✓ A brief description of who you are.
- ✓ Your role at the company.
- ✓ Your strengths (how you stand out from others).

Practice your speech with a trusted friend or colleague, to ensure you deliver it with confidence, knowledge, impressiveness, and enthusiasm. By making a memorable impression, you increase the likelihood of being remembered by your marketing target as someone they want to connect with. This speech offers an excellent opportunity to shape how others perceive you. For example, your elevator speech could be, "Hi, I'm [Name], and I'm passionate about driving results. As a [Job Title] with (x) years of experience, I've consistently exceeded my targets, streamlined processes, and collaborated effectively with cross-functional teams. I can immediately impact your organization and help you achieve your goals. I'd love to discuss potential opportunities and learn more about your company." If you can identify something unique about the other person and provide a positive comment, they might be more likely to remember you. For example: "By the way, I understand your daughter was just accepted to the University of Texas in Austin. Congratulations to her! Texas is my alma mater if she has any questions."

Tuning your elevator speech to your target is important, especially when attending a client/customer lunch or event. You want to speak to your client's specific needs and establish why they should choose you or your company for new business. Work your target by tailoring your speech accordingly. "It's about telling your story in a way that showcases your strengths. It's a way of building a bridge to others and better opportunities."[1]

As you take on more responsibilities at work, make changes to your elevator speech that showcase these new or expanded skills, highlighting your abilities to lead and manage teams. For example, you could say: "Hello, my name is [Name]. *I am a results-driven leader with a proven track record in managing high-performing teams.* As a [Job Title] with x years of experience, *I have developed an in-depth understanding of motivating, developing, and empowering individuals to achieve personal and professional success.* I'm confident in bringing *my leadership skills* to your organization and driving team and business performance to new heights. I'm excited about the opportunity to discuss how *my expertise in leadership and management* can benefit your organization. Thank you for this opportunity."[2]

Crafting and maintaining an effective elevator speech is crucial for advancing your career. You need to develop this communication tool early to succeed throughout your professional endeavors.

Get to Know and Appreciate Your Clients, Customers, and Vendors, and Add to Your Network of Contacts

Prioritize your clients by treating each one as though they are your only customer. Satisfying their needs to the best of your abilities increases the potential for future business with them or other clients they may refer to you. According to statistics, obtaining referrals can be lucrative for businesses, depending on the nature of your business.[3] Referred customers can bring 25% higher profit margins, 18% more loyalty, 37% higher customer retention rate, and are 4 times more likely to refer more customers.

However, you must build trust and credibility with your clients before requesting referrals. Developing a strong bond with a client will make your client choose to work with you on future endeavors (including if they change companies or start their own business). Cultivate relationships with those you work with, whether colleagues, customers, or vendors, to capitalize on future networking opportunities. Professional connections can lead to unforeseeable pursuits and more business. You never know how newfound connections may help you someday.

You can achieve building trust and credibility in working relationships by consistently delivering high-quality services, maintaining open and transparent communications, demonstrating expertise and knowledge in your field, and showing empathy and understanding toward the needs and concerns of the persons you serve. Additionally, providing transparent and honest advice, respecting client confidentiality, and being reliable and responsive can help establish trust and credibility. See more tips on how to establish a rapport with your clients later in this chapter.

Identify New Targets for Marketing Purposes—Once a Week

Making an effort to connect not only with the people in your office, customers, and vendors of your company but also with potential targets outside of your industry strengthens the reputation of your capabilities and marketing experience.[4]

As noted, devote time each week to building and maintaining your network of potential and existing contacts for business. Send a note or email, schedule a lunch or drink after work, or plan a dinner. For in-person meetings, consider including a colleague who might also benefit from an introduction, and can speak to your respective experiences. Any new contacts you make that positively contribute to your company financially will help present you as someone who adds value in the eyes of management, benefitting your career growth and earning potential for future promotion.

Working Your Target

To make a good impression on a potential client, spend quality time in advance researching their business and industry. Create talking points to share how you and your company can add value to them. When you meet, take mental notes on their interests (professionally and personally). After the meeting, maintain detailed notes for each contact, including relevant information that will aid in recalling important details about them. Ask where they are from and what brought them to their current job. Where did they go to college? Do they have kids? Try to know some personal information about your targets by discovering their educational background, hobbies, job positions, and relevant personal interests. Determine if you have any common interests or noteworthy relationships. You can differentiate yourself from competitors by establishing a personal connection before making a business pitch.

For example, compliment their work if the target has written a book or article. If you see an article or any information related to them, their work, or their industry, send it to them with a personal note. Additionally, remembering their children's name(s), what interests them personally, or subjects that grab their attention is also an effective way to build rapport. These are great ways to break the ice with a new client, showing that you are a thoughtful person who cares about them, not just their business. If your efforts translate to work, "treat them like they are the only client." They will appreciate the attention and care you provide, increasing the likelihood of them returning for future business opportunities.

Once you've established a strong rapport, explain to the potential client why your company is the one to hire by outlining your experience, success with similar transactions, and how your approach is more efficient—including from a cost perspective. Explain how your team cares more than your competitors. Be prepared to support your opinions with statistics, examples, and proof. Create a written, detailed proposal plan completed with an estimated budget (and how you communicate adjustments to the budget) for extra support. Make sure your proposal is both professional and personalized to your target. If you have a marketing department, let them help craft a perfect pitch. Your marketing folks are a valuable resource you should take advantage of.

Your proposal should offer an overview of how you will deliver the product or complete the project as a supplier or provider. Ensure you mention essential details on how to avoid common challenges and unforeseen expenses (you can do this by consulting colleagues, researching, or pulling from your own experience, if relevant). Impress your client with your proposal, but keep your strategies private. Share enough ideas to spark interest in your company's unique approach. Highlight any add-value efficiency measures to showcase your expertise and differentiate yourself from competitors. For example, describe how you intend to manage your team to ensure efficiency for time spent and costs incurred, including regular reporting on status to the customer/client.

Additionally, promoting diversity within your team is an important selling point that will likely give you an edge over competitors. Many companies require a team populated with women and minorities to foster diverse and inclusive work environments that offer a variety of perspectives and innovative ideas.

To summarize, it's important to research and tailor your proposal to each target client's unique needs, personality, and goals to differentiate your pitch from competitors. Carrying this out will require investing your time, research, and resources to develop a personal and unique proposal and to assemble a suitable team. These endeavors will likely lead to valuable rewards as your marketing efforts pay off, and your company recognizes your contributions to their success. Ultimately, you can establish a reputation as someone who enhances the value and profitability of the company.

Developing a Personal Relationship with Your Client Is Key

Building a personal relationship with your client is a valuable tool to promote customer satisfaction, loyalty to you, and a commitment to your company's services. "90% of CEOs believe that customers have the greatest impact on their business... 80% of customers say they are more likely to do business with a company if it offers personalized experiences."[5] More notable: "Companies that provide an emotional connection with customers outperform the sales growth of their competitors by 85%." Id.

Management will value your efforts to foster ongoing positive relationships with existing clients and customers.

Establishing a personal relationship with your customers allows you to understand their needs and preferences better, which can help you provide them with more personalized and effective solutions. The moment your client views you as a trusted advisor and friend, they will be more willing to have open discussions about sensitive issues, including the project's importance to their career, company, or potential outcomes of failure. Having a personal relationship can also make it easier to address any challenges or adjustments needed to complete the project successfully.

Building personal connections with customers fosters trust and loyalty towards your brand or business. When customers feel valued and understood, they are more likely to be satisfied with your products or services, leading to repeat business and positive word-of-mouth recommendations.

To strengthen your relationship, meet your client outside the office in a casual setting, such as a dinner or happy hour. This relaxed environment can help your clients feel more comfortable and open to sharing personal information or concerns, which can help you understand them better and ultimately improve the work you do for them. Further, the positive development of this relationship will result in your client holding greater trust and confidence in your work.

Avoid Being a "Know it All;" Instead, Foster Trust

To effectively communicate with your client, you should avoid patronizing or acting like a "know-it-all." People could read these behaviors as arrogant and dismissive, which can alienate clients or customers. Lecturing, humiliating, or shaming them (especially in front of others) is equally unappreciated.

Instead, focus on being clear and concise in your communication style. Allow your clients to express concerns, listen actively without interruption, and show empathy to build strong relationships and provide effective solutions. Building strong relationships with clients can lead to business success in several ways. It fosters trust, loyalty, and repeat business. Satisfied clients are more likely to refer others to your business, leading to new opportunities and growth. Additionally, strong relationships allow for better communication, understanding of client needs, and the ability to provide tailored solutions, which can set you apart from competitors.

These approaches can help to foster a positive and effective working relationship with your client.

Ask for Introductions and Referrals

Marketing is crucial for most businesses' success and can occur internally and externally. Take a proactive approach to opportunities by going through your contacts weekly and planning to meet or call someone who could potentially provide introductions or referrals for your career growth. Feel free to ask for help or support from these people. The worst that could happen is that your target says "no." If that happens, don't give up. There may always be another opportunity.

When you receive an introduction or referral, show gratitude by sending a thank-you note or a small gift. Going out of your way to show your appreciation can foster positive relationships and potentially lead to more future opportunities.

Using Social Media (The Do's and Don'ts)

According to statistics, 84% of employers are recruiting via social media.[6] Social media plays a significant role in hiring and retaining employees in today's working world. Knowing these facts, your contributions on social media should be thoughtful and mindful of the impressions you are presenting of yourself and your company. Be professional!

When using Facebook, LinkedIn, or Twitter, you must be mindful of the photos and opinions you post and interact with. Avoid posting content that could harm your reputation or cause others to question your values, behavior, or brand. Once something is posted online, it's difficult to remove it, so exercising caution is key. Additionally, it's important to be aware of any job responsibilities or company policies regarding social media that could potentially affect your online activity. Potential customers and future employers may scrutinize your social media presence to evaluate whether you fit their company or brand. Therefore, taking an active role in managing your online reputation is crucial.

Protect Your Turf

It's important to celebrate and communicate your marketing successes regularly. This includes informing colleagues and superiors about your accomplishments. By doing so, you can ensure that your hard work is recognized and avoid the risk of someone else taking credit for your work. I experienced this early in my career as a young lawyer, and I quickly learned to speak up. Failure to report your successes can lead to misunderstandings about who actually generated new business, potentially hindering your progress in your organization. If your contributions are unclear, it's important to clarify who is responsible for the project's success. In this way, you can ensure that you receive credit for your achievements and continue to advance your career.

Once you are successfully developing new work from existing clients of your company, you should be receiving accolades or rewards (such as bonuses) for maintaining and generating business from those clients. If former clients or customers of your company come back to hire you later for new business, fight to receive credit for the new business generated. Speaking up is important, especially when your salary is dependent in part on the business you generate for your company.

Learn how to stand up for yourself and your team by openly sharing achievements with your superiors, highlighting team accomplishments in meetings, and giving credit where it's due.

Consider scheduling regular one-on-one meetings with superiors to discuss your progress and accomplishments. Prepare a concise summary of your and your team's achievements, highlighting specific results and their impact on the organization. Be confident and proactive in sharing your and your team's successes, and provide any supporting evidence or data to showcase these contributions. To advocate recognition, gather information and evidence that demonstrate the impact of your team's work. Present this information clearly and persuasively to decision-makers, emphasizing the value and benefits it brings to the organization. Build alliances and relationships with key stakeholders who can support your cause, and be persistent in making your case. Additionally, consider leveraging internal communication channels to highlight your team's achievements and generate visibility.

If you collaborated to successfully bring in new businesses with others on your team or within your company, share the credit fairly. Doing so will foster respect and trust with your colleagues.

There were times in my career when a partner of mine would quiz me on how I generated a new client business, only for me to find out later that he found a way to use the information I shared to take credit for my success. In one case, the mere fact that he was my superior and had a contact with the same company as my new client was sufficient to take the credit in the eyes of management. I became aware of my superior's communications when management came to discuss the state of our office and met with each partner personally. In my private meeting with management, I found out this superior was taking credit for some of my newly generated business, completely disregarding my efforts. I informed management how I brought in and expanded the new client and reclaimed the client. Afterward, I resolved the issue with my superior partner.

I was fortunate to have wonderful superiors who taught me the best ways to generate new clients and business for the firm. This particular partner was one of them; however, he did not recognize how his self-serving actions were potentially affecting my career growth and compensation at the firm. I emphasized the importance for him to promote and support the growth and potential of those coming up the ranks behind him, including vocalizing the proper distribution of credit for new client business to management at our firm. He was receptive to my concerns, although he did need to be reminded from time to time to be respectful and fair about the hard work of others, especially the younger members of his team or in his division.

It's essential to communicate and clarify the source of business and achievements to make sure everyone understands who is responsible for marketing successes. In doing so, you can promote an environment that encourages growth and fair distribution of credit while avoiding potential hindrances to career growth and compensation.

7

Find Your Voice and Toot Your Horn; Be Visible

Speak Up for Yourself; Be Assertive

Studies indicate that women hesitate to assert themselves or speak up in the workplace out of fear of being labeled negatively. This assertion proves particularly true when discussing one's accomplishments at work. Women who "toot their own horn" are often viewed as unattractive or unlikable, especially if they come across as "too assertive." However, by actively sharing accomplishments and successes at work, women can challenge these stereotypes by demonstrating their value.

Don't be afraid to 'toot your horn' loud and clear. Men do it all day long without repercussions. If done respectfully, you will heighten your visibility within your organization, especially in conjunction with promotions, raises, and other professional opportunities—leading to recognition from colleagues and industry peers. More importantly, by sharing your successes, you become a role model, advocate, and mentor for young women in your field. Self-advocating not only benefits you in your career but also helps others build confidence in their abilities and navigate the challenges they face in the workplace.

To be successful in any field, you must be confident in your skills and abilities. Furthermore, your peers and superiors must hear and observe this confidence. Tooting your horn helps you recognize your achievements and builds the confidence to take on new challenges and opportunities. However, you must be bold. It is very important to speak out and stand up for yourself. Before you know it, 'tooting your horn' will become second nature. Please do not rely on others to do it for you.

Make Yourself Known during Meetings

When you attend a meeting, make every effort to participate sensibly. "While many women stay quiet during work meetings to maintain a kind, courteous reputation, by not asking questions, they are doing a disservice to themselves and their work progression."[1]

If the meeting is informational or relates to a new project, ensure you listen carefully, take notes, and actively participate by asking thoughtful questions relevant to the subject. According to research by the Harvard Business School, "those who ask questions and seek advice are seen as more competent by their peers than those who remain silent." Id. Similarly, if the meeting involves instruction on a new subject, research the topic before the presentation to be more knowledgeable and prepared to participate.

During discussions, write down key points you would want to use to organize your thoughts. This will help you make a smooth delivery. If the leader asks for any remaining comments after the meeting, don't be afraid to speak up and return to a prior topic to contribute.

Showcase Your Abilities and Successes

Be prepared for any meeting, especially if the subject matter lies within your expertise or you have been asked to present on a topic related to your field. To bolster your contributions, have your key facts and arguments ready. You can do this by rehearsing your points beforehand, including responses to any anticipated questions or challenges. Be succinct and firm in your delivery. Speak confidently and share appropriate, credible backup information to support your position. Preparing makes you more knowledgeable and bolsters your credibility, building respect among your co-workers. Additionally, if you know of trusted co-workers or superiors who know your points of view in advance, encourage them to support your position. By demonstrating your preparation and knowledge, your colleagues will be more likely to listen the next time you have something to say.[2]

Foster your expertise on a topic by volunteering to give presentations to senior folks at the company, writing articles or papers on the subject, or giving speeches to your clients, customers, and industry groups. Becoming an expert in your field is a positive way to earn your peers' respect and promote career progression.[3]

Don't forget to advertise your recent presentations, publications, and project successes in meetings, on your company's website, with customers, clients, trade associations, and women's social networks. Taking these actions lets you highlight your expertise and contributions to the company and community. If you have mentors or sponsors at the company, ensure they are current on your achievements so they can promote you and your work as opportunities arise.

How to Impress When You Are Working Remotely

According to a recent study conducted during the COVID-19 pandemic, several gender gaps emerged for men and women working remotely. 34% of men with children were promoted, over 9% of women with children, 28% of men were assigned important projects, over 10% of women, and overall, only 29% of women felt working remotely positively affected their career over 57% of men.[4]

Working from home can hinder establishing solid relationships with colleagues and superiors, impeding opportunities for desirable assignments and recognition for outstanding work. Working from home also limits face-to-face interactions, making seeking feedback and expressing interest in desired tasks difficult. Phone calls also lack the nuances of in-person communication, making it challenging to accurately interpret reactions. As a result, women, in particular, must focus on increasing their visibility, building rapport with colleagues, and making noteworthy work contributions to impress their superiors.[5]

Here are some suggestions: First, get a feel for your company's culture through video conferencing calls or telephone conferences. Are calls more formal, requiring specific work attire and advance agendas with formal requests to speak on issues, or are they more casual with respect to attire and agendas? Where guidelines are lacking, consider dressing to impress and request to be added to the meeting agenda on a topic of interest, helping you to stand out and be noticed. Are call times limited where you must adhere to established schedules? Especially if you are a new hire, you do not want to hold a reputation as wasting anyone's time by unnecessarily elongating discussion topics. Prepare to research any questions/concerns you have to limit extending past the designated meeting time. If needed, ask for additional information regarding work assigned by colleagues by contacting them outside of scheduled calls, especially if you notice the company's call culture does not encourage "off-point" queries. You want to appear efficient and respectful of everyone's time and the company's style.

When leading a project, gather progress reports from each team member before meetings. This effort enables you to report on accomplishments and attribute credit where deserved efficiently. When working independently, summarize your progress and successes, highlighting how your contributions add value to the company. Reach out to colleagues in your area before the call to encourage their support during your call.

Building colleague relationships is crucial to enhance project productivity and promote professional growth. To achieve this, schedule one-on-one conversations with each team member, focusing on a common interest or relevant topic. Allow sufficient time for a personal connection while still respecting any schedule limitations. To show genuine interest in your colleague's work, start the conversation by referencing their contributions in a recent meeting. This engagement proves that you pay attention to your colleague's ideas and respect what they say, which they will appreciate. During the call, take notes on personality traits and specifics you notice for each person to find shared interests and other unique topics you can follow up with when you speak with them again. These efforts demonstrating your genuineness and authenticity will strengthen your relationship with your colleagues and bolster their trust in you. They are then more likely to support you during calls. As for your work product, do more than your superior requires. Focus on delivering high-quality results that meet or exceed expectations. Most importantly, complete tasks on time and ask for feedback.

Whatever you do, refrain from appearing overzealous. Respect your colleagues' boundaries and preferences for communication. Additionally, request call times and "follow-ups" during normal working hours unless suggested otherwise by targeted participants. This increases your likelihood of receiving positive recognition and appreciation when you reach out later to resolve work-related issues or request project assistance.

Pay special attention to colleagues and superiors who know people who are critical to your company's growth and try to build relationships with them. These individuals can act as influential sponsors or mentors for any goals you wish to achieve.[6]

Mastering Self-Promotion

As we have noted, women who speak about their achievements often face negative stereotypes that label them as less likable, unattractive, or, in some cases, as "show-offs." These assertions cause women to refrain from promoting their work, hindering their advancement. Google diversity programs specialist Julia Silva said that "Our role is to be humble, and the hard work will pay off." Female employees are expected to work quietly, regardless of any lack of advancement, and trust that their efforts, though unacknowledged, will eventually grant promotion.[7]

By contrast, men frequently brag about their accomplishments without fear of backlash.

Accordingly, to combat the negative sentiments instigated by these stereotypes, master a more subtle way of promoting yourself by highlighting your accomplishments to your superiors and colleagues (men and women) respectfully and positively.

Use Past Accomplishments to Your Advantage

Find a context where your personal accomplishment effectively adds value to the group or company. "By the way, I wrote an article on [TOPIC] just published in the ____ Trade Journal. I have extra copies if you want to send some to your clients interested in the company's expertise in this area." Using past accomplishments for the benefit of the company or group demonstrates how your relevant intelligence and contributions advance the company's expertise.

Highlight Positive Actions You Have Taken

Another way to illuminate your noteworthy efforts: "I found a new client opportunity for our group, and we will meet with them tomorrow to see how our company can help them with a new project they are contemplating." Or, "We just closed our first transaction with [new client] under my leadership, and the client has promised more work will come our way."

Communicating positive actions you have taken informs your colleagues how your efforts benefit the team and the company.

Find a way to keep your colleagues and superiors regularly informed on your activities before someone else tries to take credit for your efforts. Even as a young associate or member of your team, take advantage of any opportunities to make yourself known among colleagues and superiors. For example, if you notice a subject matter relevant to your group needs an expert on the topic, let your group know you plan to research the subject and create a presentation to educate them on your findings. As you make successful presentations, your reputation as a dedicated worker and an expert on the subject will spread positively throughout your company.

Women must learn to self-promote and do so loudly to be seen, heard, and rewarded for their efforts. However, in doing so, research suggests that we must master the crucial balance between sharing successes while refraining from triggering negative stereotyping from our male (and female) peers and superiors. Meaning, if women brag gracefully with some humility while highlighting their accomplishments, they are more likely to be heard and taken seriously. Bottom line, you may be overlooked for new opportunities or promotions if you don't share your successes with your superiors. Additionally, once you have established a reputation for your accomplishments, you are more likely to be respected when you have something to contribute.

Sadly, some women hold biases against women who "brag" about their work accomplishments. Please resist, and if you see other women exercising biases like this, confront that attitude. Self-promotion should not warrant negative feedback if you present your accomplishments respectfully and truthfully. Please keep track of your achievements via a document and practice how you present them to a trusted friend or colleague. Add any notable accomplishments to your elevator speech when speaking about your role within the company or during the first introductions. Also, empathetically make an effort to champion the work of others around you when deserved, especially around male colleagues and superiors. Speaking up for others bolsters respect for who you promote and yourself as a supportive, dedicated group member.

Go the Extra Mile

One way to gain your colleagues' and superiors' attention is by *going the extra mile*. Doing this means volunteering for tasks that exceed your job parameters. However, be careful not to overwhelm yourself. Taking on too many tasks at once will only cause inefficiency and stress, consequently risking weaker results.

For example, if you are available during busy times, ask your colleagues or superiors if they need assistance on any project, especially if you notice them struggling. Take on extra projects or tasks, even those that may not fall within your work description. Don't hesitate to work outside your regular group and comfort zone. Using your unique talents and perspective to assist others and contribute to their projects will rouse interest from your colleagues and superiors. You will establish a reputation as someone who exceeds expectations and someone people can count on. This reputation as a valued, contributing employee will foster your career growth and promotion within the company.[8]

Managing Workloads; Setting Work Boundaries

Some work environments, especially start-ups, are stressful until a proper definition and designation of responsibilities occurs. If a colleague or supervisor abruptly leaves, the person left behind often takes on the departed person's responsibilities until the company hires someone new, which can take months. If more people leave and no replacements are hired, the workload for remaining employees increases to an unbearable extent. This overwhelming workload often comes without proper rewards or salary increases.

If your work assignments outweigh your pay grade and responsibilities, please speak up and ask for appropriate salary adjustments. Surely, your company values you as an employee and will agree to accommodate you. You can say: "[Boss], in addition to my full load, I am also handling the work of Sandy and John, who recently left the company. To keep up, I am working most nights and weekends. Please consider adjusting my salary to compensate me for my increased responsibilities. *[Suggest a salary range, if possible.]* However, we must hire another person to pick up an appropriate amount of their workload as soon as possible. I would be happy to help interview for this replacement."

Set a firm timeline for your pay increase and replacement hire under the consent of your superior. Managing your workload by firmly maintaining your responsibility boundaries makes your job less stressful, ultimately garnering the respect you deserve from your coworkers and superiors.

If You See a Teaching Moment, Take Advantage!

If a hug, a hand on your back, or a kiss on the head makes you uncomfortable, let the offender know immediately—gently, if possible, or with a bit of humor. We all have different comfort thresholds for human touch and likely heightened sensitivity if the violator is a stranger or a superior. It doesn't matter if the violator is from an older generation who claims to not 'know any better' or a violator serving as a boss or superior.' No one and I'm emphasizing that NO ONE is excused from any physical behavior that makes you uncomfortable; such behavior has never been okay or acceptable. It may have been tolerated for fear of repercussions (such as loss of raise, promotion, or job) or fear of punishment or violence, but it has NEVER been okay. The #MeToo movement made strides to educate and force changes in the law. Your body belongs to you, not to anyone else, no matter their age or position within the company. If you feel uncomfortable, stand up for yourself and use the opportunity to educate your offender. Especially in today's environment, your immediate education of inappropriate behavior should warrant appreciation from the offender—you will have potentially kept him out of trouble and you will have drawn a firm line of respect.

For example, we agree that some behavior may seem innocent, such as someone leaning over you as you work on the computer. However, if that person feels 'too close and personal,' say something like: "You're in my space!" Use a light-hearted voice and smile to avoid the violator taking offense and thus reacting harshly. If he places his hands on your shoulders, say: "Too close and personal!" If he seems confused at your response, tell him that touching makes you uncomfortable in a casual, non-threatening tone. Maintaining this balance between calling out the violator light-heartedly while still ensuring they understand the inappropriateness of their behavior is vital to keeping your reputation positive when dealing with issues like these.

If the behavior continues, communicate more firmly with the violator. If your message continues to be ignored despite your efforts, remove yourself from the situation and seek help from someone who influences their behavior. If all else fails and the behavior persists, file a complaint with HR.

Any unwelcome touching is never appropriate—especially in the workplace, no matter how 'innocent' the behavior may seem. Remember that your job position does not include receiving touches from colleagues. Your work environment should make you feel comfortable and safe. Addressing inappropriate behavior immediately helps the violator understand your concern and learn from their mistakes. For many violators, this immediate confrontation and education regarding inappropriate behavior saves them from engaging in such actions later, where the repercussions of such violations could be detrimental to their career and reputation.

Don't Tolerate Interruptions, Stealing of Ideas, or Disrespectful Behavior:

> Meetings with Colleagues

Imagine you are in a meeting populated by a majority of men. Despite your efforts to contribute to a topic of your expertise, your male colleagues continuously interrupt you, speak over you, or ignore your attempts to participate altogether. Even a senior female employee at the meeting says nothing to save you from these unfair intrusions. The situation becomes more frustrating when a male colleague repeats and takes credit for your idea, which the group then praises. This scenario may be familiar to many.

Let's review some examples of how to address these situations appropriately:

First, remember that you earned your seat at the table and hold every right to be heard, regardless of gender or minority status. You deserve to be fully respected as an equal member of the team. The next time someone cuts you off, take a deep breath, stand up, and get the group's attention. "Hold on, folks! I have something to say." Once you command the attention of your colleagues, share your ideas. If a colleague tries to interrupt you again, raise your finger—signaling for him to wait until you are finished. Tell him, "Wait, I am not finished! You are welcome to speak when I am done." Be firm but gentle in your declaration. If you smile while putting him in his place, he may not take offense and hopefully realize his disrespectful behavior.

Standing up for yourself takes courage, especially if the interrupting colleague is your superior. After you do it once, it will get easier to do it repeatedly. Just remember not to apologize for speaking up. You are not asking for a personal favor to share your opinion. Add that your idea is in the company's or your department's best interest for greater impact. Be confident, not invisible. Work actively in meetings and conversations to share your valuable and worthy opinions. Before you know it, your willingness to stand up for yourself will become second nature.

If a colleague repeats your idea as his own, interject and clarify to the group that it was your idea. Stand up if you need to. You could say, "Wait, that was my idea! I just made this point a few minutes ago!" To certify your statement, provide:

- ✓ Immediate detail on what prompted your idea.
- ✓ The impact on the team or project.
- ✓ The cost to the company.
- ✓ The ultimate benefits.

Back this explanation with evidence, data, and other research to bolster your credibility and integrity. If applicable, compare your previous ideas that helped the company or your team. By appropriately claiming credit for your idea and leveraging the opportunity to showcase your prior contributions, you can establish trust and credibility among your colleagues and superiors in the meeting.

During a meeting, if a colleague blatantly takes credit for a report you prepared or a project you completed or an idea you presented to him, you must find an opportunity to speak up and defend your efforts. Interject, saying something like, "Coming back to the work John described, I actually prepared those reports to help John," providing specific details about the purpose and benefits of the reports to underscore your claim in completing them. Suppose there is no appropriate opportunity during the meeting to clarify the work as yours; pull the violator aside afterward. Remind him that you prepared the reports and that he should reasonably attribute your contributions in the future to support your career. Follow up by sending a clarifying email to the group and copying the violator on the message. "John asked me to clarify that I prepared the reports and to direct any questions regarding details to me." If you are worried, the violator might retaliate, alert a supervisor.

➢ Meetings with Clients or Customers

You are in a meeting with a male customer and your colleagues, and the subject of the meeting falls under your area of expertise. Despite your efforts to engage with the customer, he refuses to make eye contact with you, uses a disrespectful tone, and insists on responding only to your male colleagues in the room. After the meeting, this customer follows up with a male colleague to complete the transaction, ignoring that you were the appropriate person to contact. In a different scenario, the male customer refuses to take you and your professional expertise seriously during the meeting. Instead, he continuously makes objectifying comments about your looks and states that he would like to go on a date with you, embarrassing you in front of your colleagues, potential clients, and/or superiors.

In both cases, you pose as the victim of disrespectful behavior. Your customer may not believe that women are capable experts in comparison to men or deserve equal respect to men. So, how should you respond?

If your customer exhibits demeaning behavior, such as refusing to maintain eye contact with you, take a moment to inform the customer of your expertise and encourage your colleagues to certify your abilities. Direct your customer's attention to you in a gentle but firm manner. "Paul, may I please have your attention? I need a few minutes to walk you through my expertise on this subject." If necessary, knock on the table to make the customer look at you. Clarify that you possess higher knowledge on the subject than your colleagues, certifying you as the expert for the product or transaction. Once you have gained your client's full attention and established your credibility, return to the subject of the meeting.

By showcasing your abilities in a firm but gentle manner, you draw a professional line of respect while simultaneously resisting putting the customer on the defensive. How might your colleagues' step in to help you in the above-noted situations? Before the meeting, ask a male colleague to "have your back." Ensure this colleague is willing to confirm your expertise, great character, and similar project experience with the customer. This input on your proficiency from your colleague reassures the customer that through your work together, they will be in good hands. Men will listen to men. Research has shown that having a male colleague speak positively about a woman's abilities can help counteract negative gender stereotypes and biases.[9]

Shockingly, I had an experience with disrespectful behavior from a female client of our law firm who stubbornly ignored me and instead focused all of her attention on my male colleagues. It took an extra effort to gain her trust, set her mind at ease, and prove that I was not looking to outperform or compete with her. I intentionally asked my male colleagues to show up late for a planned dinner to alleviate any friction. This action gave us valuable time together without any of my male colleagues present, allowing her to genuinely get to know and bond with me without the pressure of a work setting surrounded by businessmen.

If your customer makes inappropriate or demeaning statements, especially ones specific to your gender, let him know that your presence pertains to helping strictly with product advice—not personal matters. Ideally, your colleague, especially a superior one, should intervene gently with disrespectful clients, reminding them that 'flirting' or 'looking for a date' is not the purpose of your presence.

If your colleagues say nothing when inappropriate behavior occurs, ask for a quick break and use it to discuss these concerns with your colleagues privately. Educate them on the importance of resisting bystander behavior and ask them nicely to talk to the customer about his or her inappropriate behavior. Use the example of, "What if you were their sister, wife, or mother?" Surely, they would not want her to be treated in such a disrespectful, objectifying manner. Let your colleague walk back into the meeting first—and alone—to give him time to privately address your concerns with the customer, saving them from potential, though well-deserved, embarrassment.

➤ Remind Colleagues Not to Be a Bystander

Ask your male colleagues to have your back! If they witness a female colleague facing constant interruptions and demeaning comments during a meeting (whether in person or online), they can use their position to speak up effectively. Educate your male colleagues on behavior that is not acceptable and offer them appropriate phrases they can use when intervening. For example, it is okay to say, "Hold on, let Julie speak and finish her thoughts." or "Julie is not here for your personal pleasure, and your comments are making us all uncomfortable. Let's keep this professional!" Teach your male colleagues not to act as bystanders but to use their male privilege in the work environment to improve the experiences of female employees at the company. If applied respectfully and with a genuine effort by the male colleagues, this method will prove incredibly effective and make for a more productive and healthy work environment.[10]

Getting to know your male colleagues personally and bonding with them facilitates relationships, making them act as allies in supporting you when needed.

➤ Support Your Female Colleagues

As a woman, advocating for female colleagues is crucial for enhancing your work environment. Speaking up for other women promotes a more diverse, inclusive, and equitable environment, encouraging women from diverse backgrounds to share their perspectives and ideas in the workplace. When people with different perspectives and experiences collaborate, they are more likely to develop new ideas and approaches to problems. It also helps to create a more balanced and equitable workplace where everyone feels valued and respected.

Promoting each other increases productivity and job satisfaction, improving employee retention rates. Supporting your female colleagues can also increase creativity, improve morale, and provide career advancement opportunities for everyone. Additionally, research has shown that organizations with more gender diversity tend to perform better and have higher financial returns.

Furthermore, this advocacy and support prompts male colleagues to consider diverse perspectives and avoid dominating discussions—improving gender equality and ensuring that talented and capable women receive deserved opportunities and fair treatment.

Conquering the Dreaded Performance Review

Hopefully, you are invested in the company where you work—meaning you worked very hard to get your job and care about the company and your career. If these statements are true, your performance review is an important opportunity for you to understand your current status and future development within the company. Are you on track for a promotion? Do you need to make any personal improvements to mature through the ranks? Your superiors use the performance review to evaluate your progress, share any reservations regarding your activity, and suggest changes you need to make to stay on track for promotion.

Use your performance review to speak up for yourself and ask questions. Be proactive and take control! This is your career and your future. Candid communications with superiors regarding successes, goals, and expectations promote a healthy growth environment and a successful career at your company. If needed, advise how your role has changed and your responsibilities have expanded, which now require a commensurate salary adjustment and potential promotion.

➤ Preparing for Your Performance Review

First, take the evaluation process seriously. Understand your job requirements and conduct a self-evaluation to determine if you are satisfying expectations. Identify any knowledge or resource gaps that require training or management assistance to return to your promotional track and advance your career. Keep a record of any contributions to transactions and matters you worked on over the past year (including any speeches, seminars, and other programs you may have given or helped organize). Use this record during your performance review to promote your contributions and accomplishments in an organized, professional manner. In your record, include any marketing efforts, courses, or seminars you took to strengthen your knowledge, any work opportunities you took outside of your area of expertise to help on assignments, and any additional endeavors you participated in to get to know other colleagues. These efforts will demonstrate how you have gone above and beyond your expected work requirements. Propose your plan of action for self-improvement during your review. If you have been performing above your level and taking on new responsibilities with established successes, edit your job description accordingly and communicate how your job responsibilities have expanded. If your job has drastically changed, you have a persuasive case for a raise and promotion. These efforts show how you add value to the company and are determined to succeed.

If you received written or verbal accolades from customers, colleagues, or superiors, ensure you mention them during your performance review. If available, provide a copy of these accolades to underscore your credibility. If you contributed significantly to larger transactions, ask your superior from those matters to provide his or her compliments in writing for you to share with management. Pick superiors who know you well and care about your progression in the company to conduct these evaluations. Endeavor to include any superiors outside of your work area who you assisted in project emergencies and who applaud your efforts. Keep management updated regularly on your accomplishments, positive reviews from superiors, and any new skills training you receive throughout the year. Be bold about your efforts and successes by tooting your horn. You know your male colleagues will not hesitate to do the same. Don't resist opportunities to champion your efforts by being modest.

Stay calm and attentive if you receive negative feedback during your performance review. Ensure you understand what changes you must make and commit to adjusting accordingly. Ask for clarification if needed. Additionally, provide defensive reasoning for your work if you believe the reviewing supervisor neglected important facts governing your work contributions.

Persevere if your project fails or you receive a bad performance review. Acknowledge what went wrong and look for ways you can make necessary changes to improve your performance. One of my favorite sayings about mistakes is, "You can pick up a mistake and carry it as a burden, or you can set it down and use it as a steppingstone to greatness." [Author Unknown]

As you progress, remember that you should complete every project you undertake to the best of your ability. It only takes one superior with a negative impression to impact your reviews and future at the company, potentially causing devastating consequences. If a superior expresses dissatisfaction with your work product, try to understand their project requirements and meet with that person. Gently demand the feedback you need to understand expectations and commit to making the suggested improvements. Be kind, respectful, and courteous in your communications.

Finally, "quid pro quo" is never acceptable! If your superior asks for sexual favors in exchange for a positive review, promotion, or raise, he has violated the law. For more information, visit us at www.thesandboxseries.com and read *Play Nice*.

Negotiating Your Salary

Does it surprise you that men discuss their salaries with managers four times more often than women and that 57% of women claim never to have negotiated their salary?[11,12,13]

Even more astounding, when applying to the same job, women ask for a lower salary than men 65% of the time and often accept the first offer they receive (as opposed to men who continue to negotiate upward).[14,15]

Additionally, six times out of ten, women are paid less than men for the exact same job at the same company. On average, this salary difference is 3% less.[16] According to reports, women typically earn less than men, currently 84 cents on the dollar, and would need to work 42 days longer every year to earn the same amount of money.[17]

The New Yorker put it this way: "Today, for every dollar American men earn, American women earn eighty cents. This means that American women effectively work from January 1 until March 15 without getting paid."[18] Over a 40-year career, women stand to lose $400,000 because of that wage gap.[19]

This wage gap looks even greater when you break it down by race and ethnicity. "While women of Asian descent earn eighty-seven cents on the white-male dollar, black women are typically paid sixty-three cents and Latina women fifty-four."[20,21,22]

Latina, Black, and Native American women will average making $1 million less than white men over their careers, despite doing similar work.[23] At current rates, America will not close the wage gap until at least 2059.[24] This translates to smaller social security checks and much less retirement savings for these minority women.

To combat this unfair discrepancy, help your company or target employer bridge the wage gap and prepare yourself before you negotiate your salary.

➢ Do Your Research

First, do your research and determine the pay range in your area for similar jobs. Check online resources such as Glassdoor, LinkedIn, PayScale, and BLS (Bureau of Labor Statistics).[25]

Many companies burden you with setting salary expectations without offering any transparency on their salary ranges for your job position. This unfair practice may cause you to accept a salary only to realize later that you are underpaid in comparison to your peers. Unfortunately, it could take years for you to catch up financially, depending on the company's annual percentage raise practices. Luckily, there is a growing trend to combat pay discrimination in the workplace by implementing pay transparency laws designed to remove the historical secrecy around pay information. These new laws require employers to disclose, either in job postings or upon request, salary ranges, health care benefits, other insurance options, retirement benefits, leave policies, as well as bonuses, commissions, stock options, and profit-sharing. However, only a few states have enacted such laws to date, including California, Colorado, Connecticut, Maryland, Nevada, New York, Rhode Island, and Washington.[26,27] While certain states do not have pay transparency laws, companies with remote workers in any of the above states subject to wage transparency laws might be required to comply. Id. Depending upon the state, non-compliance could result in enforcement action, fines, or civil penalties.

Pay transparency laws are forcing companies to study national databases to determine actual industry standards prior to posting new job salaries. While transparency may lead to potential poaching by other companies and salary renegotiations by current employees, it can ultimately result in equal pay and competitiveness in the job market. Greater transparency can also improve communication with management and reduce employees' concerns about being underpaid, leading to a focus on job performance and opportunities for career advancement. This benefits everyone involved.[28] By contrast, a lack of pay transparency risks losing talented employees.

The enactment of these wage transparency laws has already shown an increase in the average hourly wage for Colorado—11.5% since January 2021.[29]

Championing transparency with respect to pay scales, salary structure, and promotion would help ease the pressure of negotiating salaries and raises, ultimately making your company a better, more profitable work environment.

For example, France took proactive measures to close the wage gap in 2018. In France, men were being paid 9% more than women, on average, even though equal pay has been the law for more than 45 years. Under a new law, companies with more than 50 employees have three years to eradicate pay gaps or face fines. These companies must install software in their payroll systems to monitor unjustified pay gaps.[30]

We hope this common-sense proactive measure taken by France to protect against gender disparities in the workplace, will inspire other influential nations to implement similar legislation.

If your state's practices fall behind in terms of other state's legal transparency requirements, arm yourself with data on salary and resource info that explains why you deserve your requested salary. For certain jobs, at least for the first several years, you may not have to go to such lengths. At large law firms, for example, salary information for the first few years is readily available. Firms are always competing for the best associate candidates and typically will publish their salary structures to stay competitive.

➤ Avoid Stating Your Current Salary

If asked, avoid stating your current salary. If pressed, note that your current salary needs to be updated to meet current market expectations. In California, Delaware, Massachusetts, and the cities of New York and Philadelphia, it is now illegal to ask a job candidate about his or her salary history—a practice considered discriminatory to women.[31]

Fairygodboss expertly described in a recent article: "As a candidate, it's better to be asked about your salary preferences than cornered into revealing your current salary. But it's ... tricky...it's easy to lowball yourself and regret your answer. The last thing you want is to walk away from a negotiation feeling like there was money left on the table. You shoot yourself in the foot by answering a number that was way below your employer's initial range."[32] Being prepared and arming yourself with market information for similar job positions in your area is critical in ensuring you gain a desirable salary.

➤ Create a Satisfactory Range

For example, when negotiating your salary for a new job, create a range that starts with the minimum amount you require (higher than your current salary) and justify your range by factors such as education, experience, unique qualities, skills, and the value you bring to the company compared to other candidates. To support your request, find comparable data in the market, equipping yourself for further negotiation after an initial offer is made. Remember, you have nothing to lose by negotiating. Moreover, your preparedness and efforts increase your potential to earn more in the long run. If you can justify your request with true and competitive data, your potential employer should be fine with your negotiation efforts for a pay raise. One study found that 85% of Americans who countered an offered salary were more successful in achieving close to their salary goal. Don't give up and take the first offer, especially if you qualify for a higher wage.[33]

For more on this topic, check out this article from St. Catherine University titled "How to Negotiate the Salary You Deserve."[34]

➢ Set Expectations Early

It's important to set your salary expectations early in the negotiation process to avoid any future frustration. This helps establish a benchmark for how you wish others to perceive you and your contributions. Your superiors need help to read your mind and innately understand what salary you deserve. So, it would be best if you made your desires clear—upfront.

Allowing your employer to guess what you may be seeking will not likely satisfy your expectations for a raise, leading to continued frustration. By establishing your expectations early and backing them up with facts, you put yourself in a strong position to negotiate and improve your chances of achieving your deserved salary.

➢ Don't Settle for Low

As you negotiate, don't settle for a lower salary just because you believe you lack the criteria for the job position. Instead, educate your potential employer on your personal experience especially that which extends beyond the position's parameters, to emphasize why you add value to the job position. Sell your skills, experience, unique work style, and attitude![35]

If instead of a higher salary at the number you desire, your employer offers you stock or equity in the company and/or other financial benefits, including quarterly or year-end bonuses, determine if the combined offer with these benefits bridges the gap in pay. Stock or equity in your company could be a valuable benefit in the long term.

Finally, put your pitch in writing and practice with a friend or family member who could provide valuable input on how to negotiate best.[36]

Negotiating for a Raise or Promotion in Your Existing Job

A 2018 PayScale study noted that almost two-thirds of employees have never asked for a raise.[37] According to another study, when women find out that men are paid more for the same job, only 26% complain to their manager and 6% to HR. Rather than asking for a commensurate raise, 36% leave their employment for a new job or stay silent (28%).[38] Further, the study also found that where salary discussions are initiated, 57% of men are more likely to get the pay increase versus 50% women. Instead, women are more likely to receive improved job titles, benefits, bonuses, and/or stock options (7% men vs. 10% women). Id.

We understand negotiating a higher salary is stressful—some say it may be more stressful than getting a root canal; however, don't be afraid. Even if the answer is "no," don't give up.

Ask for what you want in a percentage increase, and as you would for a new salary at a new job, support your request with your educational background, experience, unique qualities, skills, accomplishments, and comparable data for similar jobs in the market. When noting accomplishments, make sure to include any marketing successes you contributed to for new business for the company, any courses or seminars you joined to improve your expertise, and work successes, and any work opportunities you engaged in outside of your department with the intent to get to know other colleagues. All of this demonstrates your willingness to go above and beyond your expected work commitments.

Explain how your unique talents and efforts add value to the company financially, including how you resourced new customers (and, in turn, new business), shared your work with other colleagues within and outside of your department, and grew your practice or team.

These efforts show how you add value through your determination and motivation to succeed.

Speak positively about your role within the company. Give examples that describe your effective work contributions, your role in expanding the business, and your overall loyalty and dedication to the company's success. If you have been taking on new responsibilities with established successes, edit your job description accordingly to make a more persuasive case for a raise and promotion. Seek support from superior colleagues to corroborate your efforts. This effort will help you make an endorsed case for why you deserve a raise or promotion.

➢ How to Ask for a Raise or Promotion

Time your promotional request carefully, ideally after completing a significant project, achieving a major goal, or receiving positive feedback. Additionally, consider the appropriate person for the request. Is it your direct supervisor or the department manager? Will it be more effective for the supervisor to request on your behalf? Finally, do not request if your target person is under pressure at work or not in a positive frame of mind.

Consider alerting your superior that you would like to schedule a time to discuss your market research in relation to the possibility of a raise. Giving your superior the "heads up" allows him or her to prepare for the discussion as well. This upfront, respectful communication lends credibility to your request. Approach the conversation with confidence, but remain professional in your tone. As previously highlighted, prepare for any objections or questions that may arise. Speak firmly but respectfully when communicating your expectations regarding raises and bonuses. For example, "I would like a raise of __%. I have been at this company for two years, have exceeded expectations pursuant to performance reviews, and deserve this raise. What I am asking for appears in line with my research for similar jobs in our market area."

Be prepared to review your expanded responsibilities and established work successes for a more persuasive case to make for a raise and promotion. Don't be afraid to speak up for yourself. You have nothing to lose.

Additionally, when you ask for the raise, if applicable, be prepared to discuss your contributions to the company in terms of numbers. For example, to what extent did your successful work contributions impact the financial bottom line of the company? Give your superior specific numbers. Also, prove to your superior that you have done your market research by sharing factual information supporting your raise in compensation.

For any job, regardless of whether or not it is your first, you must be proactive when negotiating your salary. Only you can defend and promote yourself for the salary you seek.

In my jobs at law firms, every attorney annually submitted a memo on our successes to the compensation committee. In many cases, after this required submission, follow-up interviews took place, during which employees had the opportunity to highlight their contributions to committee members and address compensation concerns. I still remember one particular interview where a new managing partner fell under the false impression that a client I resourced for the firm was actually originated by another colleague while I was only "doing some of the work." This false assumption was made when the colleague mentioned a connection he held to my client, which resulted in the colleague receiving all the credit for the client (and commensurate added compensation). After all, how could a woman generate such a client? I picked up on my managing partner's false belief immediately. I explained how I resourced the client and grew the client's business to other practice areas of the firm, further corroborating my claim.

In a law firm setting, originating new clients (and business) for the firm is highly competitive and typically triggers an increase in compensation. Don't let a colleague take credit for your originations. Stand up for yourself and set the record straight. Later when I became a member of the firm's compensation committee as a partner, I learned how important it was to have allies on the committee who were educated on the contributions of their fellow partners and associate attorneys seeking raises.

When you receive a referral for business from another colleague at your company, ask to share the credit. Your referring colleague should receive "origination credit" for the business; however, if you grow the relationship, manage a team to complete the work, and generate additional business with that client or customer on other matters, your contributions should be appropriately rewarded. Your ability to increase the profitability of the company by sharing the work, building the practice, and marketing your company's expertise are important traits for a successful career.

Foster courteous and respectful relationships with your colleagues through open and honest communication. You may need their help to complete work and foster continued business from a client or customer, especially if the work falls outside of your area of expertise. However, don't be afraid to stand up for yourself and your contributions—even if someone else succeeds in taking the credit. Complete your work respectfully and with maturity to underscore your value, competence, and loyalty to your team and company. Your efforts will be noticed. Remember, you may work for someone who will eventually hand the reins of their business over to you.

If your request for a promotion is deferred for consideration to a later date, present a follow-up plan to keep the request on your superior's radar and keep good notes of your conversations. These can serve as future evidence for any promises made or possible discrimination.

8

Maintaining Balance at Work and Relieving Stress

Hundreds Have Preceded You—You Can Do It

Many young women spend too much time at the start of their careers worrying about how they will balance their work and home lives once they get married and have children. Although we do recommend you take note of your company's culture before you accept a job, once you start your career, focus solely on building your career and not these important personal decisions until the time is appropriate. Remember that you have likely already managed difficult time constraints while studying in school, working part-time jobs, or helping at home. You deserve a fulfilling career that reflects your hard work and showcases your dedication. Refrain from stressing too early—countless women before you have overcome similar—or worse—challenges. More importantly, know that the goal of this book is to help you navigate workplace challenges that may arise in the future.

The "30 Minute Rule"

My dad was a military man. As a result, we grew up with many rules, including a few important ones, to help us start the day on a healthier note. My brother and I would come downstairs at breakfast, and before we could sit down at the table, Dad would bark, "Are your beds made??" If not, we would run back upstairs and make our beds. While it may appear minor, this important task gave us a sense of accomplishment and made coming back to our room at night more pleasant and inviting for a good night's sleep. I think of my dad every morning when I make my bed.

Dad also enjoyed the "30 Minute Rule." This rule made all the difference in getting me to work on time and in a better mood. To help begin your day in a relaxed and healthy manner, consider setting your alarm to wake up 30 minutes before your usual time. Waking up earlier gives you ample time to get ready, eat breakfast, and prepare for the day ahead. Also, consider making exercise part of your morning routine. "Research has shown that exercise gives energy. Starting the day with 30 minutes of cardiovascular or strength training will wake you up better than a cup of coffee will" … and … "Even 30 minutes of exercise before work will leave you energized, clear-headed, stronger, and more able to take on the stress of the day."[1] In addition, according to a recent survey, a "far higher percentage of respondents who exercised in the morning or during the work day said these areas of their work improved thanks to their physical activity compared to employees who save their workouts until the end of the day." [2] By setting a healthy tone for your workday in the morning, you'll be able to start off on the right foot, feel confident, and maintain better focus throughout the day.

Ask for Help

If you find yourself working on too many projects without proper assistance, ask for help. In many cases, some employees are specifically designated to help you with certain aspects of your work, or you can recruit someone who is underutilized. Attempting to do everything alone leads to burnout and lower-quality work. By contrast, delegating certain tasks exhibits leadership skills and the ability to manage projects successfully and confidently. Asking for help is not a sign of weakness, and saying "no" to more work does not signal that you are a "bad" employee. We will review how to best address these challenges later in this book.

Take Breaks for Your Health and Career

As a young lawyer, I was hell-bent on keeping my head down and going above and beyond expectations to get my work completed perfectly. Dedication beyond the call was my code to live by, resulting in many long days and nights in the office. I did not leave before my superior, and I tried to get to the office before he or she arrived. I took very few breaks and rarely left the office for lunch or dinner. Yes, this work lifestyle was incredibly exhausting and obviously not good for my health. These standards of working are typical for many law firms and other high-stress professions. As I matured, I realized taking a walk outside to get a cup of coffee or leaving the office for an occasional lunch helped me clear my head and re-fuel for the remainder of the day. Before too long, with encouragement from some of my more senior colleagues, regular lunch outings, coffee time, or drinks after work with colleagues became a welcome break from long hours at the office. I soon realized taking these breaks with colleagues was a very important opportunity to get to know them and learn more about my job, the law firm, and my superiors. Most importantly, it was a great opportunity for others to get to know me and assess my abilities.

Take regular breaks throughout the day for your health, the betterment of your career, and to improve your productivity and focus. "94%

of employees who take breaks feel like their breaks refreshed their perspective on work."[3]

After a few years at my first law firm, my team and I would leave the office during the afternoon to grab coffee and cake at a small cafe down the street. This break gave us a chance to catch up on office transactions and discuss who needed help or a new project. Going out to eat lunch once or twice a week with colleagues will facilitate similar outcomes.

Most importantly, create opportunities for yourself by using some of your breaks productively. Is there someone in the company you still need to meet with whom you might want to work? If yes, go to the person and introduce yourself. Make time to call a potential business contact or a customer to "catch up." Meet with customers and friends for lunch, dinner, or drinks. You never know; your visit or call might open up a new work opportunity or beneficial relationship.

Organize Your Home Life (Like You Do Your Job)

Set clear boundaries between your work and personal life. Designate specific times for work and leisure, keeping separate physical spaces for work and relaxation. For example, establish a routine during the day, designating working hours, breaks to clear your mind, an hour for lunch, and allotted time for exercise. As we noted earlier in this chapter, getting up earlier in the morning to workout, eat a proper breakfast, and get ready for work will help you start the workday with a greater focus, and you avoid the risk of a busy workday derailing you from exercising or personal time later.

To maintain your work and personal life boundaries, communicate your needs and priorities with your employer and colleagues when necessary. These needs can include your schedule availability and your priority of maintaining a healthy work-life balance—especially if you have regularly planned personal activities important to you or your family. For example, my team would meet regularly at the beginning of each week to address any potential conflicts (between work and home)—this was important if we were in the middle of transactions with impending deadlines which required us to work late at night and/or on the weekends. If a member of the team needed time off for personal commitments, another team member would take over his or her responsibilities, or we would get resources from other groups at the company to fill any requirements.

Refrain from taking on more work than you can handle or accepting social work-related invitations that you worry will significantly impact your work or personal life. If workloads or conflicts between home and work become overwhelming and you feel uncomfortable addressing these challenges with the delegating parties, find a senior person you trust to help with communications or visit HR for help. Resolution is important for your mental health and well-being.

Try to avoid checking work-related emails or taking work-related phone calls outside of work hours—the operative word being "try." We recognize that for many work professions, this advice is unrealistic—the work does not necessarily stop after business hours. However, you could also work for a superior who does not respect your time outside of the office and operates under the assumption that you should always be available for a work-related call regardless of its importance. If the latter reflects your work situation and you receive a work call during your non-working hours, don't ignore the call. You can send a quick text if you are in the middle of something important and if the call does not seem urgent. For example: "I am unable to speak at the moment, but I will get back to you as soon as possible" or "when I am back to work in the morning or Monday morning, assuming the matter can wait." If the call appears urgent, do your best to respond to find out if the call can wait until you are back at work. It is better to connect and briefly excuse yourself than to ignore the call or message completely. This method of dealing with work matters infiltrating your personal time will help you mentally switch off from work and focus on your personal life. Self-care should be an essential part of your routine, including exercise, relaxation, socialization, and hobbies.

Finding the right balance between your work and personal life is a continuous process of trial and error. However, by prioritizing your needs and establishing clear boundaries, you can find a balance that works for you.

Prioritize Mind & Body; Take Care of Yourself

Stay healthy. Whether you enjoy going to the gym, playing a sport, or indulging in a hobby, take the time to work these interests into your schedule. If you exercise daily, conduct your workout in the morning to ensure its completion. Work may get too busy and stressful for you to find time at the end of the day to exercise. This routine includes small breaks as well, such as taking a quick walk to clear your head or grabbing coffee with colleagues. Going to health appointments and taking care of your family are also important endeavors that should be included in your planning process. Schedule all of these activities as you would any meeting or phone call. Don't neglect yourself or your family in order to propel your professional career. Instead, use your career to improve yourself and your family. Use your lunch break to run personal errands so you can go home as soon as the workday ends. If you are worried about uncompleted work, go to work early or work late the next day, or go home and work remotely when you have completed family tasks. Having the ability to work from home helps relieve the stress of being away from work. It allows for more quality time with your family and friends. The important part is that you prioritize your time at home and aim to return home at the appropriate hour every day.

Finally, realize that you cannot do all these things by yourself. If you are married or have a significant other, work with your partner to equalize household and childcare duties. If childcare or a nanny is not cost-efficient, resource childcare assistance from your employer or seek help from family members and friends who are interested. Good childcare grants significant peace of mind.

Maternity Leave/Mommy Track/Adjusting Your Schedule

Early in my career, more than 30 years ago, I was worried about what motherhood might do to my career path. To succeed at my law firm, I knew I had to put in long hours and work hard to prove myself to stay on track for partnership. Having children was likely to slow my progression and potentially derail my reputation for being available and reliable on projects that required 24/7 commitment—at least for a period of time. At the same time, my male peers (and husband) continued their careers without disadvantages. I did not want to give my superiors any reason to stall my goal of partnership, and I did not want any of my clients to seek alternative counsel. After all, I had worked very hard to land my job at the firm, and I was building my practice and client base. So, I decided to wait to have children until I became a partner.

That would not be my advice to myself today. Back then, I believed as a partner, I would have achieved equity and goodwill for all my hard work—a valued employee the firm would want to support and keep if I needed a more flexible schedule for a short period to accommodate maternity leave. At the time, very few of the female attorneys at the law firm had children. For many of the women who did, their situations were similarly influenced by their desire not to let motherhood affect their careers. In one case, the female partner's husband was a stay-at-home dad, which allowed her to spend more time at work. In another, a female partner decided not to tell her clients she was going to have her first child, worried her male clients might take their work elsewhere. The road ahead was definitely daunting for motherhood. When an opportunity arose to participate in creating a more progressive maternity leave policy for the firm, I volunteered. The experience was valuable and eye-opening. I can still hear some of our more turbulent discussions surrounding eye-raising questions and statements from some male colleagues: *Why do mothers need more than a few weeks of parental leave to recover from childbirth? Why should women continue their regular career path, promotions, and pay while on maternity leave (and early years after)? At the same time, their male counterparts work a 100% full schedule. Surely, as a mother, they will no longer be able to perform at the same level due to the new responsibilities they will be facing as a parent of a young child. It would be irresponsible to ask mothers of young children to work late hours, attend meetings outside of normal working hours, or work on high-profile matters that might require undivided attention or travel. As a mother, they should consider an alternate profession!*

Despite the many issues raised and often disappointing discussions, we implemented a fair maternity policy. However, we, women, were not able to change many of the opinions or concerns made by our male counterparts regarding motherhood and the potential impact on career progression. These discussions only underscored my determination to wait to have children.

Unfortunately, many of those discriminatory opinions, if not all, still exist today.

When I became a partner, my concerns about the impact of motherhood did not change. I wanted to retain all of my clients, and it was important to make sure that any of my work requirements were completed with the same quality and attention as before. When our first baby, Samantha, was born, I was expected to take full maternity leave under our law firm's new maternity policy that I helped create (six to eight weeks). Instead, my leave at home was very brief (less than two weeks). I resumed working and even completed a loan transaction for a client a few days after coming home with our newborn. Today, I would not recommend this to any woman.

I was spending too much time at work and needed more time at home taking care of Sam. It was emotionally and physically draining, so with urgent support from my husband, I started pondering alternatives. A very good friend who worked for a different law firm eventually talked me into moving to help him staff a new practice area. This move granted me more flexibility and fewer hours at work so that I could spend more time at home. Unfortunately, this transition meant I would have to join his firm as "counsel" and give up my title as a partner. It was a tough decision, but I made the change. It gave me peace of mind that I would spend more time at home with Sam and my husband.

Of course, my shortened work schedule did not last. We had started a new and exciting mortgage securities practice, which took off and became successful. Our client base grew exponentially, and with that, so did my hours at work.

When our second daughter, Nicole, was born a few years later, lack of staffing within my area of practice did not allow me to take full maternity leave. The alternative would have been to hand over my clients to a different group of attorneys at the law firm, and I was reluctant to do this. As a compromise for coming back to work early, my superiors promised that I could take the balance of my maternity leave at a later date. As you might predict, this did not happen.

Luckily for me, my clients were understanding. I chose to be transparent with them about having children and motherhood. When the time came, they were supportive and unsurprised if they heard a baby crying in the background or if I had to leave a call unexpectedly. They trusted that my team would get the job done. Before too long, I made a partner for the second time. As my workload increased, I was able to maintain flexibility with the help of a well-trained team, understanding clients, and a very supportive husband.

As I progressed in my career, I made it my mission to look out for women coming up the ranks behind me. Having a family is a personal choice and different for every person, and you may not always be able to "plan out" the timing of your pregnancy. Regardless, your company or law firm should be supportive of your choice and timing of pregnancy without any requirement to sacrifice your career progression.

I recommend taking full maternity leave for your health and your family, regardless of where you might be in your career, if your company offers this benefit. If you have a reputation as a valued employee, your company will encourage your journey. Having understanding superiors and a support group that can jump in and help during your absence is essential. Company policies that set clear guidelines for maternity leave, pay, and career progression during your absence and upon your return are very important in ensuring you are not at any disadvantage in comparison to your peers, male or female. Additionally, regular education of all employees, including executives, regarding the importance of such guidelines is equally important in order to minimize discrimination and unfair treatment of new moms upon their return. Know that many women have succeeded in their careers while becoming parents before you. You can do it!

Plan ahead for your absence. Recruit other colleagues and your team to take over when needed and return the favor when they go on maternity leave. Educate your clients and customers on your situation and when you plan to return to work to help manage expectations. Study the company's policies and benefits for a clear understanding of your rights and entitlements. Seek appropriate assurances that you will be brought up to speed on work developments and changes upon your return, ultimately ensuring that your career progression will not be delayed or derailed as a result of your absence. Meet with your superiors and colleagues to communicate your intentions to continue your career upon reentry, including work assignments and responsibilities, travel schedules, career goals, and childcare. These issues become more important depending on the length of your maternity leave.

Unfortunately, as we have noted, not all women have equal rights regarding maternity leave or work policies in their jobs that prohibit discrimination with respect to pay or promotion upon return from having a baby. In the U.S. The Family and Medical Leave Act of 1993 (FMLA) requires 12 weeks of unpaid leave annually for mothers of a newborn or newly adopted child, *but only if they have been employed for more than 1250 hours with a company with 50 or more employees*—unpaid leave. Note that for the majority of U.S. workers at companies with fewer than 50 employees, there is no legal requirement for paid or unpaid leave. This has a negative impact on women in low-paying jobs who cannot afford to take unpaid leave. A number of states have supplemented these federal regulations to either lower the company-size threshold or provide longer leave periods with pay. Many companies in other states (without such legal requirements) have followed suit. For example, some of the largest law firms around the country allow extended maternity leave for an additional three months or more, with the first three months fully paid.

If you choose to take maternity leave (whether extended or not), you want to be sure you are fully re-acclimated to your job responsibilities, and you review them with your superiors upon your return to manage expectations. If you hold a management position or are a partner, planning ahead of time will be even more important. You will want your team to be fully prepared to handle the work and manage expectations with minimal oversight from you during your absence. However, you should be able to check in and manage from a distance as needed.

There is no question that motherhood while working is a challenge. Plenty of research suggests that the majority of household chores and responsibilities of raising children continue to fall on working moms in dual-career couples. Add to that the constant guilt of missing out on your children's important milestones, school events, extracurricular activities, or doctor's appointments, or neglecting your own self-care and missing time with your partner, friends, and family. If you feel overwhelmed and are tempted to quit, don't do so until you have fully considered the potential long-term consequences. There are alternatives.

Sara Holtz said it best in her recent book "Advice to My Younger

Me": "...taking time out of the workforce for child-rearing [risks] lost income, lost wage growth, lost promotional opportunities, and lost retirement benefits throughout your career...Then, once you reenter the workforce, the [pay] raises you receive over the remaining life of your career will be based on the diminished salary you will likely earn when you go back to work...Over a lifetime, you will earn considerably less than you would have had you stayed in the workforce continuously." The bottom line is that a lengthy absence from the workforce makes it more difficult to return to a comparable position and salary.

You will have to decide what is best for you and your family. Personally, I enjoyed the stimulation and challenges of my job, the opportunities to learn and grow in my profession, the gratification of success, and the comradery with my colleagues and clients. It was important for me to have both a family and an ambitious job. To do both, I had to make sacrifices—and it wasn't always easy. I learned how to schedule important personal matters like work appointments and work remotely from home after hours if I needed to catch up on assignments missed during the day. I set up a home office so I could work remotely without missing a beat. This was critical if I needed to be home for my kids, and returning to the office would not be efficient or healthy.

Most importantly, however, I married a guy who learned to understand my challenges with lots of love and patience and stepped in or resourced alternatives when needed. We both had to learn to adapt.

One important personal story comes to mind. Not long after Samantha was born, my husband expressed concern over my late hours at work. He could see I was struggling emotionally from having to work late. Frustrated, he asked, "Why do you have to continue working through the night after a long day at work? Doesn't the firm understand you are a new mother?" Fully appreciating his concern, I thought about how best to respond so he would understand my challenges. I asked him, "What did you do before you left the office today?" He pondered and said he was on a lengthy conference call with his attorney, who was providing comments to finalize an important contract that needed to be signed by the business folks the next morning. "Was it Elizabeth, the one with two young children?" I asked. He confirmed, realizing that he had asked her to work late. Her husband was likely asking her the same question. Elizabeth could have said no to my husband's request to have the contract ready the next morning; however, she likely felt like me. Satisfying the client's expectations and important timelines for work matters is an important priority in fostering a successful legal practice. Saying "Sorry, no can do" is not always a realistic option. This example helped my husband understand that the same was true for me.

As I became more senior, I had greater control over my schedule, and I learned how to manage work assignment expectations for myself, my team, and the clients.

If being overwhelmed at work is a regular occurrence, don't quit before you consider alternative work schedules. If none are available at your company, look for another job that has more flexible working hours. Many companies now have "part-time" or "mommy tracks" for promotion or partnership to help with any concerns about keeping up with early parenting responsibilities during the first few years after childbirth. Flexible "remote" options may also be available. When you are ready, you can then return to a full-time schedule. However, be wary and do your research. Find out if these alternatives have been successful for other colleagues who have chosen this path. You may find that your career could be derailed for years to come. Remember the concerns I described above while I was serving on the maternity leave policy committee? Being "part-time" might exacerbate these types of concerns. You will likely be working just as hard as if you had remained full-time—for less pay.

You may not have to change to a "part-time" or "mommy track" position if you are a hard worker with a successful track record at your company, honest and transparent with any conflicts or childcare issues, reliable, and an overall good employee. In today's environment, you can work remotely and be home when needed. Doing this may mean you will have to work a few late nights after the kids go to bed, but you can do it. Remember, hundreds have done it before you, and you should not be penalized for adjustments you make after having children.

Take Advantage of Company Benefits (Mental Health, Childcare, etc.)

These days, many companies (60% plus) offer moderately inexpensive childcare benefits, such as Dependent Care FSA; however, they are often not well publicized and need to be more sufficient to help families make childcare affordable. In contrast, only 6% of U.S. companies offer significant childcare benefits, which on average can cost $12,000 or more annually (depending upon location), according to a new report by Clutch.[4]

Familiarize yourself with your company's policies on parental leave and childcare benefits, including the amount of time off, pay structure, and eligibility criteria for paid leave and benefits. Determine if they are lacking and noncompetitive in your market area. If you are looking for a great resource to compare company policies, @theskimm launched a database sharing the paid leave policies of 500+ companies and growing.[5] If childcare benefits are relevant for your family and a good percentage of your colleagues, encourage your company to bolster or add these benefits, ranging from childcare subsidies, on-site childcare, backup childcare assistance, to flexible childcare spending accounts. Speak up and advocate for changes to your company's parental leave policies. Allowing parents to choose more flexible work schedules and remote work opportunities is another helpful benefit to accommodate childcare needs. Id. Join forces with other employees who are also passionate about these issues. Working together can increase leverage and make your voice more powerful. Stay up-to-date on changes in your company's policies regarding paid maternity leave and keep the conversation going with management and HR to ensure that the policies are constantly evolving to meet the needs of new and expecting mothers. Companies that offer better childcare benefits have greater work morale and are thus more likely to attract and retain talented professionals—making them more competitive in the marketplace. "That's because parents view childcare benefits as a sign that the company cares for them and their families, and this increases loyalty." Id.

The same applies to mental health benefits. "It is illegal for an employer to discriminate against you because you have a mental health condition," says Arielle B. Kristan, an attorney with employment law firm Hirsch Roberts Weinstein.[6]

You can't be fired, denied a promotion or forced to take leave because of a health condition or suspected health condition. Id. Under the Americans with Disabilities Act, employees with a mental condition that "substantially limits one or more major life activities" have the right to certain accommodations—such as an altered work schedule, remote work arrangements, or time off for treatment.[7] "By having senior management talk openly about their commitment to addressing employee mental health and backing up that talk with significant action, organizations can help employees feel more comfortable seeking the support they need…"[8]

Access to childcare can boost productivity by allowing employees to concentrate fully on their work without concerns about their children's care. Similarly, mental health benefits can improve employees' mental health, leading to better work performance. Providing childcare and mental health benefits can enhance the company's reputation in the community, improving its image among customers and other stakeholders.

Companies should prioritize making mental health resources easily accessible and affordable. By approaching mental health with empathy and prioritizing it, companies can help employees feel less isolated and more supported, particularly working mothers returning to work after maternity leave. One effective way to achieve this is for senior employees to regularly communicate and promote company resources, highlighting the significance of seeking necessary care for improved well-being and job satisfaction. The involvement of female leaders, particularly those who share their own experiences, is essential for female employees who may fear being perceived as weak or unprofessional for seeking help.

Though offering childcare and mental health benefits may seem expensive at first, the long-term cost savings can be significant. Healthier employees mean lower insurance and healthcare costs, while childcare benefits can reduce absenteeism and turnover.

Take advantage of all your company offers and join forces with like-minded colleagues to enact change if improvements to benefits are warranted.

9

Fostering Respect in The Workplace

The Golden Rule Regarding How to Treat Others

You would have heard the Golden Rule: *Treat others as you want to be treated.* Not only is this rule applicable on the playground, but it is also incredibly important to remember within your work environment. Being disrespectful and burning bridges will not help your long-term career. You never know where the person subject to your poor behavior will end up—he or she could be your superior someday.

If you are the boss, you don't want to be known as difficult, unpredictable, emotional, a screamer, or bitchy (especially if you are a woman). Female superiors who are known for these traits are generally disliked and criticized for their disrespectful treatment, especially when it's towards other women.

Some believe these severe traits are encouraged by the work environment. A heavily male-dominated environment may mean that top spots are rare for women, causing fierce competition among female candidates and resulting in the women being perceived as bitchy and cruel. In these environments, male bosses are preferred, as it is deemed "socially acceptable" for male professionals in power positions to demonstrate such severe traits. By contrast, senior women who display these behaviors are deemed unattractive, bitchy, and difficult to work for.

Workplaces populated with female leaders and more women in the ranks ease the competition and make the women working there more relaxed and friendly.[1,2]

We believe in Marrone's statement: "Agreeableness is not a weakness, and kindness is not a vice. Women who treat others fairly and ethically tend to both be happier people and more productive employees."[3]

I have seen my fair share of difficult female leaders in male-dominated environments who, despite their controversial traits, I ultimately respected and admired; however, as I have noted, I don't believe you have to talk, dress, or act "like a man" to get ahead and be successful. There are a number of alternatives, positive traits you can adopt that will be beneficial to your success, which I review in this book. You don't want to be non-approachable or feared to such an extent that you are not respected as a leader. Your followers should want to work with you, learn from you, and trust in your leadership style and abilities.

Set a high standard for compassion and respect, and don't give anyone a reason to disparage you—colleagues and superiors alike.

The Impact of the COVID-19 Pandemic on Working Women:

> The Clock Has Turned Back on Gender Equality and Discrimination

The outbreak of COVID-19 turned the clock back on gender equality for working women. In many cases, the lockdown pressured working moms to give up their jobs or work remotely, often at reduced pay, to handle important child or elder care duties, homeschooling, and household responsibilities, causing a dramatic increase in anxiety, depression, and sleep loss among women. If this wasn't enough, working remotely subjected women to increased gender discrimination and inappropriate comments for "staying home to take care of mommy duties." To make matters worse, coming back to work post-COVID-19 after losing a job or a cut in pay means it will take time to make up the loss in salary—risking the loss of financial stability, retirement income, and future growth.

Studies indicate that women have been disproportionately affected by COVID-19, as 40% of all working women suffered the most job losses (compared to 36.6% of men) across a variety of industries, including food, hospitality, retail, and real estate.[4]

Data released by the Bureau of Labor Statistics disclosed that 865,000 women (age 20 and older) left their workplace in September of 2020 compared to only 216,000 men. This data confirms a disturbing trend that could set back gender equality in the workplace for years to come.[5]

According to another source, men have regained their job positions lost because of the COVID-19 pandemic. In contrast, "While women gained 188,000 jobs in January 2022, they are still short by more than 1.8 million jobs lost since February 2020. It would take women nearly 10 months of growth at January's level to regain their lost jobs, the NWLC report indicated."[6]

It is well established that in two-income households, mothers are more likely to carry the majority of household responsibilities, including cleaning, laundry, grocery shopping, cooking, childcare, eldercare, and furnishing the house.[7] A study of more than 6,000 heterosexual North American couples found that working moms who earn more than their spouses still shoulder more of the housework, contradicting the conventional notion that the partner who works less carries the bulk of the domestic load.[8]

The COVID-19 pandemic made matters worse. Many women were forced to leave their jobs for childcare and elder care responsibilities during the pandemic. Schools and childcare facilities were closed, third-party in-home child and eldercare was scarce, if not non-existent, and the women who traditionally managed and/or shouldered these responsibilities had no choice but to stay home. Working remotely while juggling these important duties wasn't worth the effort or the income to justify staying on the job.[9]

"The pandemic's impact on women and women of color, in particular, threatens women's economic security in the future," Emily Martin added. "This country is really facing fundamental questions—whether we're going to make long-term investments in childcare, paid leave, and paid sick days that help ensure that caregiving responsibilities don't have this terrible economic impact."[10]

CBS 11 reported on Sunday, October 4, 2020, that during the 'new normal' of COVID-19, 80% of women took on the chores and schooling in their households over their male partners. Thus, in the wake of the pandemic, not only did women work from home, but they also performed their nanny's and children's teacher's jobs. The stress of juggling all these tasks caused a dramatic increase in anxiety, depression, and sleep loss among women.[11]

Ultimately, at the height of the pandemic, the unfortunate conditions forced many women to make difficult decisions. Either quit their jobs to stay home and take care of children or, where allowed by their employer, move to a reduced work schedule with much less pay, risking their financial stability and future growth. As a result of the COVID-19 pandemic, women may lose their future financial security if their employers restrict their ability to return to a full salary, detrimentally affecting their potential for retirement income and pension wealth.[12] A recent AARP survey noted that post-COVID-19, 25% of women ages 50 to 64 are not confident that they will have sufficient savings for a comfortable retirement. AARP also found that women retire with a staggering 30% less in savings when compared to men.[13]

In two-income households, men typically have more choices of either returning to work or staying home to deal with chores and take care of their children. Traditionally, this domestic role falls on the woman. "Though the COVID-19 pandemic necessitates the need for many men and women to work from home, recent literature arising from the pandemic suggests that women continue to disproportionately bear the responsibilities of unpaid care work at home, such as taking care of children and the elderly."[14] Large studies of adults in the United Kingdom found that women spent far more time on unpaid care work than men during the COVID-19 lockdown and identified being female as a predictor of stress and depressive symptoms, with place and pattern of work having a greater impact on women.[15,16]

"Possibly the greatest risk for women regarding future developments in the workplace may be the solidification and widening of gender gaps in pay, productivity, and job satisfaction; if employers continue to adopt working from home as a primary mode of work, evidence suggests that without the provision of adequate support by employers, such as flexible schedules, childcare support, and work assignments, workplace inequalities between men and women may continue to widen."[17]

Post pandemic, challenges persist for many women who continue to work remotely, especially if they have young children and other distractions at home. If her spouse or partner has returned to the office, interruptions during video conferencing calls are likely.

You would expect your colleagues, superiors, and clients to be understanding and patient with the inevitable distractions resulting from your circumstances. Unfortunately, according to reports, the COVID-19 pandemic requirement to work from home triggered a dramatic increase in gender discrimination against working women.[18]

It was not enough that women were already at a disadvantage by being expected to sacrifice their careers by either quitting their jobs to stay home with their kids or negotiating a cut in pay to stay home and work remotely to take on the stress of juggling job and childcare responsibilities. Virtual working prompted an increase in the frequency of inappropriate comments, such as "We are excluding you from this new project since you are too busy with mommy duties," or if the employee asks her superior for help and the superior dismisses her concerns, stating, "You will just have to deal with it to keep your job" or "If you can't adjust, your career will suffer." These discriminatory comments only serve further to ostracize women from their already detached work environments.

Now, more than ever, it is important for employers to take every precaution to prevent the persistence of such discriminatory behavior in the future.

Unfortunately, due to the fractured nature of present work environments (remote vs. in-office), companies monitor compliance with policies that protect against bullying, discrimination, sexual harassment, and racism less actively, triggering indifference and hostility from senior employees against working moms. Often, in a remote environment, supervisors largely dismiss or ignore employees' complaints about inappropriate comments made by superiors or colleagues. In many cases, the complaining employee eventually faces termination in retaliation for making complaints, though officially documented as "for business reasons" or "for failure to perform her job duties."

As a result, working moms worry about sharing their work-life challenges with colleagues out of fear of judgment. Additionally, they stress over potentially receiving negative feedback on their work because they have childcare responsibilities.

> Protect Yourself from Objectionable Behavior by Colleagues or Executives

If you work from home, take detailed notes of any discriminatory behavior you experience. Violative behavior includes restrictions when participating in a call because your children are present, exclusion from important meetings and calls because "you have too many important mommy duties," or declarations that you lack the eligibility and focus to work on a project based on the assumption that "you will be busy with your family." Comments about the fact that you have children or about your "mommy appearance" are discriminatory. There are cases where the superior kept scheduling essential work calls during lunchtime despite an employee's continuous objections that the time interfered with her important childcare duties. If you ask for relief and your request is dismissed with "you will just have to deal with it or quit your job" or "if you can't adjust, your career will suffer," recognize that these dismissals are discriminatory violations that you should report to your HR department.

Working mothers have traditionally battled systemic workplace biases, exemplified through hiring, pay, and work experience discrimination. Research shows that motherhood is the strongest trigger for bias. Women with children are 79 percent less likely to be hired, only half as likely to be promoted and earn much less money than women with identical resumes who do not have children.[19] We believe a male employee with children would not suffer from this type of bias. Employers must make every effort to stem the tide of workplace gender equality worsened by the COVID-19 pandemic.

> ➤ Remind Your Employer about the Importance of Supporting Working Mothers

Obviously, the COVID-19 pandemic created challenging times, but largely overlooked are the repercussions the pandemic perpetrated on working women. To combat these issues, remind your employer of the importance of focusing on the health, prosperity, and productivity of all their employees, especially mothers working from home. Otherwise, the employer risks losing talented women with growth potential and future vital leaders to your company.

As noted in *Play Nice*, gender diversity within teams and corporate management dramatically benefits a company's success and profitability.[20]

Employers who appear non-supportive of female employees or who act disrespectfully during challenging times are less likely to attract and retain talented employees.[21]

➢ How Can Employers Help?

If you and other female colleagues face gender-based challenges in the workplace (remote or not), brainstorm collectively on improvements your employer can make to provide proper support. The responsibility of ensuring employees feel comfortable falls under your employer's domain. The burden of dealing with inappropriate behavior or uncomfortable situations should not completely fall on the employee. Here are some helpful ways to support female employees:

Suggest regular interactive sessions with employees and leadership to reinforce zero-tolerance policies against bullying, harassment, and discrimination of any kind. Review recent violations to ensure clarity and understanding during these sessions.

Find out if your employer takes submitted complaints by employees seriously. Your employer should address any concerns immediately and effectively, conducting thorough investigations and imposing appropriate punishments for violations.

Ask your employer to provide support to employees struggling with balancing work and home lives, including in-home assistance or other options for childcare and schooling, flexible work schedules (with temporarily reduced hours during challenging times), mental health counseling (if needed), and emergency loans and grants.[22]

If you work remotely, ask your employer to provide you with the necessary equipment to complete your work efficiently.

To help with any parenting responsibilities, ask your employer to review with superiors the importance of setting realistic work schedules and deadlines—including the scope of necessary work to lighten responsibilities (for example, low-priority items should be scheduled for a later date).

Request that HR members or supervisors with proper training regularly attend teleconference calls to monitor compliance with company policies against discrimination. As an employee, if you worry about complaining to HR, don't be afraid to raise your concerns first with a superior who understands your complaints. Have him or her help you communicate the discrimination if you are still concerned about retaliation. Take detailed notes of the dates and occurrences of objectionable behavior and any witness accounts. Ask those witnesses to help you corroborate any instances of discrimination. If you need help with tips on working from home, surf the internet for advice and check out my blogs on the subject at www.thesandboxseries.com.[23,24,25]

Finally, educate your male employees not to be a bystander if they witness bad behavior. Request that they offer to be an ally to the target or complain about the violator independently to a supervisor or HR. In many cases, if they know the abuser personally, they can help resolve the behavior by raising their concerns with that person directly. Would the violator want his daughter or wife to be subject to such discrimination? We think not.

Is There a Silver Lining for Working Remotely?

According to recent reports discussing men working from home during the COVID-19 pandemic alongside their working wives, studies indicate that working men have acquired a greater understanding of the inequalities women face working from home in comparison to men. Such inequalities include the challenges of balancing paid work with unpaid work typically performed at a more significant percentage by women (household chores, childcare, and homeschooling). Working from home during COVID-19 also allowed men to learn the importance of relieving burdens of unpaid work at home to support their spouse's career; to build better relationships with their spouse and children while spending more time at home; and the opportunity to connect on a more personal level and build trust with colleagues on teleconferences, sharing juggling experiences and providing emotional support.[26]

The COVID-19 pandemic increased men's understanding of the challenges working women face due to gender discrimination. This understanding led many male superiors to work alongside their female coworkers to restructure workplace policies, practices, and systems to promote greater gender equality.

Furthermore, the pandemic brought long-term occupational benefits for both genders, including increased flexibility in work schedules and the normalization of remote work for those who need it.[27]

Women Supporting Women

Women do not necessarily champion other women. Why is that?

Throughout my career, I have met many senior women who have endured a tough road to achieve their success. In male-dominated environments, women are few and far between, especially among the senior ranks. Statistics generally show only 20% of women are in the C-Suites, and women and minorities continue to trail in compensation for equal jobs. Women have to work much harder than men to prove their capabilities and gain the trust of their superiors. The women who have worked hard to progress through the ranks stacked against them don't necessarily want other women to reach their same working level by taking an easier path, explaining one reason why women don't support other women in the professional environment. Additionally, we have heard of the "Queen Bee Syndrome," where senior women behave in ways more typical of men to display "toughness" and to "fit in,"… believing part of their success is to convince men that they aren't like other women."[28] "I am not like any woman. I care about my career" is a common comment by those embodying this syndrome, implying that if you exhibit feminine traits, you are not serious about your career.

There is also the belief that if you are a woman with influence, helping women over men might harm your reputation and standing in the eyes of senior male management—consequently potentially harming your career. You might be viewed as pro-women and anti-men, even though your goal is simply to achieve equality for women in the playground of the workplace. Female professionals may be less likely to support or promote their female colleagues to protect their own seniority status.

As a result, these women are defensive and protective of their turf (including their clients, team, and work methods). They are always concerned about possible competition and raiding of clients by other colleagues (male or female). Spending time to mentor and train women outside of their immediate, trusted circle is not likely to be a priority for these senior females—especially if a woman attracting attention for her eager attitude and intellect appears threatening. Where senior positions for women are few and far between, women who feel threatened don't want to risk the competition.[29]

I heard of one senior woman who would not allow any subordinates or colleagues to communicate with her customers directly. All communications had to be approved and run through her. Either she was experiencing competency issues with her subordinates, or she was worried that if any of her subordinates left for another job, they might take her customers with them. Another senior woman executive could not stand female competition. If another female received accolades for her successes, this senior woman would find a way to point out her deficiencies in a public forum to help dismiss her as a threat. Sadly, no one would call her out for her bad behavior. Suppose you work hard and continuously prove your undying loyalty to these senior women. In that case, you might—and I am emphasizing *you might*—eventually get these senior women to support you as a valuable ally for your future growth at your company. However, suppose you make a mistake or take any action that might be perceived as disloyal. In that case, your female superior will not hesitate to end your career—permanently. I have seen it happen.

These senior women are often described as unattractive, tough as nails, bitchy, mean, and "man-haters" with a chip on their shoulder; however, can you blame them for their attitudes? They worked very hard for years to overcome constant bias and discrimination and, in their minds, had to be very tough to survive. If they are now hard and difficult, who is to blame? Many of these women were important trailblazers who paved the way for the younger female generations, providing critical guidance for building careers. For example, at one of my law firms, a senior female partner developed one of the first all-women retreats to host existing and potential female clients, encouraging her female colleagues to foster important client development opportunities for new work. She was known to be tough and, at times, difficult; however, her reputation as a top producer and exceptional lawyer allowed her to forge groundbreaking changes for the women at our firm and later for women generally in the legal industry.

I have seen my fair share of difficult female leaders and respect their paths to success; however, as I have noted, you don't have to talk, dress, or act like a man or be a jerk to get ahead and be successful.

It is hard to believe that women would hold a fierce bias against their own gender. Former Secretary of State Madeleine Albright said it best in a keynote speech at the Celebrating Inspiration luncheon with the WNBA's All-Decade Team in 2006: "There is a special place in hell for women who don't help other women." Joyce Benenson, a psychologist at Emmanuel College in Boston, thinks "women and girls are less willing than men and boys to cooperate with lower-status individuals of the same gender; more likely to dissolve same-gender friendships; … more willing to socially exclude one another,." and more willing to destroy the career of a female colleague. Benenson believes some women are naturally competitive and not willing to provide any help to another woman that might give her or her children an advantage.[30]

One study showed that female workplace bullies targeted other women about 70% of the time."[31]

In a recent example, an elderly female in her 70s described me negatively to others as "too woke" for writing *Play Nice*, which, among other things, discusses protecting against sexual harassment. I was surprised to hear this characterization from a woman—especially given the topic of protecting against sexual harassment. Worse, this woman and I have never met, and she has not even read the first book *Play Nice*. Why would she call me "too woke?" Is she not concerned for any of her female family members or other female friends in her life? Did she not experience sexual harassment or gender discrimination in her personal life or career? Raising awareness and education on important issues like sexual harassment is necessary to create a safer and more equitable society. This issue is not political but a human issue, and we believe everyone has a responsibility to address it. After pondering, I decided to view being called "woke" as a positive and direct my critic's attention to the contents and message of *Play Nice*—how it can help both individuals and organizations deal with sexual harassment on the spot and ultimately create a more equitable workplace for both men and women. The efforts of *Play Nice* to combat bad behavior are valuable and significant, and I will not let misguided criticism deter me from pursuing the book's goals to help other women.

We have all experienced some form of discrimination or bullying from another woman, whether it is a comment about your clothes, dismissing your ideas in public, excluding you from an important meeting or lunch, or any other effort made to minimize your successes or potential competition. Compliments such as a simple "Well done!" "Congratulations" or "You look great" are rare because if these women feel threatened, they are not happy. My best advice is to stay respectful and true to yourself. Your violator may be insecure, jealous, or having a bad day. However, speak up when needed and don't let any person get away with an inappropriate comment—whether directed at you or someone else. When dealing with senior women, find opportunities to get to know them and allow them to get to know you. Eventually, you will earn their trust and be able to speak your mind more freely. Hopefully, as your relationship grows, you will have found an important new ally and supporter.

Women need to learn to support other women throughout their careers to encourage the population of women along the ranks and in leadership. Women's voices and ideas should be heard, and they should receive the training and opportunities needed for promotion. We must educate our male colleagues to support these efforts. More women in leadership will pave the way for other women to succeed and rise through the ranks, and as we already know, will help the bottom-line profitability of the company for which they work.

Many men in senior management continue to hold biases that women are not capable of working as hard as men and are not likely to become as successful, especially if they are seeking to have a family or are already moms. If women are successful, some men even believe they are more likely to have either slept their way to the top or inherited their success from a male superior. JR remembers a number of situations where male colleagues criticized her for hiring a female rather than a male attorney to handle a new work matter. When she challenged their criticism, all she got was, "You should give it to a man. That is how it is!"

"How is what?" JR would exclaim. JR says it was exasperating. Women have to work twice/three times as hard as men to obtain an opportunity. In contrast, men are handed opportunities all the time. To be acknowledged, women must toot their horns for every success and often multiple times. In comparison, if men toot their horn once, they are often deemed competent and successful regardless of what they may do afterward.

We must educate our male colleagues to support women in their organizations. It is well documented that women are better organized, detail-oriented, and patient with the micro details and day-to-day issues that arise in work matters. Women are hands-on, better managers, and more responsive. They are gentle in their approach and comforting. Women also get the job done with respect to every detail and take the time to solve issues, even after the project is completed. Women are willing to do more and spend the time—often too much time. If a new deal is on the horizon, or a transaction is commission-based, men typically have already moved on, are hard to reach, and are less responsive. We discuss the topic of the value of women more in-depth in Chapter 10.

Encourage inclusivity and diversity in senior management by highlighting the potential value that women bring to the table. Address harmful stereotypes about women's work ethic and success, especially related to family obligations. Promote transparency and merit-based evaluations to counter narratives about 'women sleeping their way to the top' or benefiting from nepotism. Foremost, promote education and understanding among colleagues to build a more inclusive work culture.

I experienced bullying and difficult behavior early in my career. As I progressed, I made it my mission to be supportive and encouraging of my female colleagues and subordinates. I was equally supportive of my male colleagues, especially minorities. In my law practice, I made a point of populating client transactions with women and other minorities, highlighting my efforts to senior management. As my career progressed, my efforts were rewarded by my firm and appreciated by our clients. Nowadays, certain clients make minority staffing a requirement for law firms to get the business.

Toxic Work Environment

A toxic work environment is one "where employees find it difficult to work or progress in their careers due to the negative atmosphere created by coworkers, supervisors, or the company culture itself."[32] Toxic workplaces can lead to stress, burnout, depression, damage to your self-esteem, and severe disruptions in your everyday life.[33]

How can you determine if you are in a toxic work environment? There are several telltale signs:

People at work are too afraid to speak up during meetings or for themselves outside of meetings due to intimidating leadership (male or female) who do not value input other than their own. Leadership is narcissistic and disrespectful, is not interested in the opinions or concerns of subordinates, and does not support collaboration, feedback, or creative freedom.

There is a lack of work-life balance. Leadership calls and emails its employees at all hours of the night and expects immediate responses. Meetings and calls are scheduled by leadership outside of regular working hours, and working on the weekends is often made a requirement without rewards or nods of appreciation.

Successes of employees are not celebrated. Decisions or rewards do not seem merit-based and only people who agree with leadership or praise them are promoted. Employees are often overlooked or forgotten even though they are an integral and productive part of the team. Layoffs are frequent, and employees do not stay for more than a year, which gives the company a high turnover rate.

Coworkers lack enthusiasm, energy for their job, and are generally not happy.

There is a lack of trust in management/leadership and generally low morale. Employees suffer from mood changes for the worse and experience anxiety and depression when they go to work. Employees and their home lives are suffering, including mood swings, trouble sleeping, weight gain, and withdrawal from friends and family.

What can you do if you find yourself in a toxic workplace? Communicate directly with the person who is creating a toxic work environment for you or your group. Set boundaries by speaking up and communicating directly, responding "no" gently when appropriate, asking for help when needed, and practicing self-care.[34]

For example, if you are constantly asked to work outside of regular working hours, ask if the tasks requested can wait until you return the next morning (or Monday after a weekend) and commit to completing the work promptly. If you are already under the gun with competing projects, inform your superior and let them know you currently have a conflict but will jump on the project once the other is complete. Some industry jobs do not allow for this type of response, given the outside pressures of customer-imposed requirements. Simply saying, "No, I am off the clock," might harm your career prospects. Working for a law firm in commercial real estate or litigation, or on Wall Street are good examples. Working at a hospital or in the emergency room is another example. If you are worried about your situation or potential retaliation, talk to your superior or a senior person who influences the violator. If that is not possible, talk to HR about your experiences and propose a plan for improvements.

As a young lawyer, I often received competing projects from different superiors, each demanding that their project be completed first and often with very unreasonable time deadlines. With the advice of trusted colleagues, I found the courage to have my superiors prioritize their projects amongst themselves and say "no" respectfully if my plate was already full.

If your superior is difficult and refuses to help you with conflicting assignments, document your experiences with the superior when you have an opportunity to review him or her with management or HR. Senior management needs to understand and resolve challenges their employees may be facing. If you are worried about retaliation, find one or more kindred spirits at work or a trusted senior colleague for support and collaborate for possible solutions. You might find a superior who you trust with influence over the violator to help resolve your concerns. Most importantly, make time for positive and healthy interactions after work to help you unwind from a stressful day.

Finally, if you don't see things changing, find another place to work. Know, however, that the grass is not always greener. If your current job is one you would like to keep, roll up your sleeves, find someone who can help, and make a plan to propose changes.[35]

➤ My Personal Experiences Practicing Law

You would think legal environments would be free of bullying, gender discrimination, sexual harassment, and other bad behaviors. After all, we are lawyers, bound by ethics, and charged to enforce and comply with the law. Unfortunately, law firms are not immune from instances of bad behavior—especially larger law firms with hundreds, sometimes thousands, of attorneys and employees. The legal website Above the Law's "The Pink Ghetto" series highlights, for example, how widespread sexual harassment is for the legal community.[36]

Some of the more noteworthy lawsuits in recent years involving sexual harassment and gender discrimination involve large firms such as Baker McKenzie, Faruqui & Faruqui, Holland & Knight, Pillsbury Winthrop, Shaw Pittman, Sullivan Cromwell, and Proskauer Rose. For example, Proskauer Rose in New York, who has acted as legal counsel in several high-profile sexual harassment cases, including CBS (Charlie Rose) and NBC (Matt Lauer), has itself been accused in a $50 million lawsuit filed by one of its female partners for discrimination in pay and sexual harassment.[37]

Most law firm cases involving bad behavior, however, are handled internally. As you would expect, larger law firms have policies and procedures in place to process any claims of discrimination, bullying, and sexual harassment. These incidents are typically settled quietly and hidden from the public eye. Until recently, arbitration and non-disclosure agreements were the norm.

Like women on Wall Street, it takes countless hours of overtime and years of very demanding work to become a female partner. Your reputation and the relationships you develop for business are paramount to your success. Men continue to dominate the most powerful positions (only about 20% of all partners are female). When women report any sexual harassment (or any other bad behavior), they risk the very career they have spent their entire adult lives building.[38]

I worked more than thirty years as an attorney (ten at my first law firm and over twenty years at the second law firm), achieving partnership status at both firms. The sacrifice to make partner is enormous, and your abilities and stamina are continuously tested. Client demands often require long hours, including weekends, with little sleep and no social life. Given the risks at stake at the job, your intellect and mental stability are critical for success. Worse, if you command a larger team, the stress level can be a serious challenge. These demands apply to both men and women who practice law; however, as a woman coming up the ranks, I knew I had to work twice as hard to prove myself equally capable, and more to make partner.

I learned not to give anyone a reason that I couldn't handle a project or stay late to get work completed. I built my reputation and trust with great sacrifice, dealing with difficult behavior from senior colleagues more often and more severely than my male counterparts. My stamina was constantly tested, especially during my younger years. Unreasonable project completion deadlines, multiple work assignments over weekends (even though the projects had been sitting on the partner's desk all week), and demands to cancel plans at night or on the weekends for non-urgent client matters were typical. Many weekend plans were canceled, only to find out on Monday morning that the weekend work project was not urgent. The partners knew I wouldn't say no to the work requests despite any personal commitments.

Remember my motto? Don't give them a reason—EVER. Sexist commentary and inappropriate behavior in my presence were frequent comic relief for male colleagues, as well as the occasional patronizing communications intended to intimidate and belittle.

For example, imagine being in a kick-off meeting on a new transaction with clients, and the partner asks you to make sure everyone has water and coffee during the meeting. This exact situation happened to me early in my career. I had not yet worked with this partner on a matter, and of the three other associates in the room, I was the only woman.

How about walking into a senior partner's office for a meeting with other male attorneys to see them watching a video of animals mating? Seeing my surprise, the partner says, "What, you don't have what it takes to work with men?"

As a more senior attorney, I asked a male colleague (whom I had not yet worked with before) to join a meeting with my client to assist with an issue within his expertise. After introductions, he tried to take over the meeting, implying the client should look to him for any decisions on the larger matter (which was beyond his specialty), stating, and "I am sure you prefer dealing with a man."

Those are some of the tamer examples. The intent behind this behavior was to see if I could handle the stress, banter, and inappropriate behavior. Could they shake my resolve to succeed?

There were many difficult challenges, but I have to admit, the behavior was especially difficult when it came from a woman.

Late one Friday night, a female partner asked me to work over the weekend in the office, even though she knew I had worked ten days straight, closed a transaction successfully that day, and was exhausted and looking forward to dinner with my family. According to her, the matter was very urgent and needed our immediate attention—yet the entire weekend, she was scarcely available. She did not attend to my completed work product, which I placed on her desk first thing Monday morning until late the following week.

Female superiors can be harsher on women than men, have higher expectations of women, and often won't hesitate to find fault with your wardrobe, mannerisms, confidence, and work product. I witnessed this behavior many times from some female partners towards subordinates. In my opinion, they viewed women as the weaker sex. If they could cause suffering similar to what they may have endured in their own careers, it gave them some sense of satisfaction.

As a female subordinate, finding a way to develop a bond and companionship with a female superior is critical to career progression, but as I may have noted previously, it may be impossible if that female feels threatened by her fellow female workers.

I learned how to manage challenging behavior from both men and women by speaking my mind gently but effectively—at times at my own personal sacrifice. If a female superior sees you as a threat, she is not likely to support your career growth. I stood my ground. It made me stronger and more resolute, and my colleagues respected me for doing so. My demeanor and manner of communication made a difference. I learned how to communicate without making enemies: gently and often with humor, drawing a firm line of respect.

I vowed to help younger generations learn from my experiences and encouraged hard work through respect and compassion. I chose to lead by example and reject competing with women simply because they are women.

Finally, in August 2016, the American Bar Association amended its rules of professional conduct to include new anti-sexual harassment and discrimination provisions (allowing victims to address sexual harassment and discrimination in the legal profession). Local and state bar associations have followed suit.

➢ Dealing with Bullies

"The majority (61%) of workplace bullies are bosses, according to a survey conducted by WBI. But that also means that more than a third are not managers but rather peers or even lower-level employees. In short, bullying can come from any direction in the org chart, and it can take different forms."[39]

We all have encountered bullies from time to time. There's the screamer, who engages in loud tirades to express his or her frustrations, usually in public, throwing items around and slamming doors—all with the intent to frighten, intimidate, and demean. There's the critic who cannot be pleased no matter what you do or how hard you work. He or she uses aggressive, disparaging, and humiliating communications to tear down every effort you make until you doubt your own abilities, ultimately causing your performance to suffer. There's the self-absorbed narcissist who thrives on making your life miserable by setting unrealistic and often unnecessary deadlines for work projects with little guidance, only to tell you later that you "missed the mark" and to "start over." Then there's the colleague who feels threatened by you and thus withholds important information on projects, meetings, calls, and time deadlines—designed to prevent you from doing your job and seeing you fail. They will often pretend to be your friend and ally when, in fact, they will do anything to ruin your reputation and, in some cases, your career.

As is the case with sexual harassment, bullies who are superiors often get away with their behavior if they are high performers and valuable to the company. If you complain, you may be ignored or transferred to protect the valued perpetrator.

Working with a bully can be especially harmful to your mental and physical health, causing stress, anxiety, depression, trauma, high blood pressure, gastrointestinal issues, and more.

As we recommend in our book *Play Nice* regarding sexual harassment, it is important to address any bad behaviors on the spot when they occur. With any bad behavior, whether it is yelling, sending ugly emails, hiding information, or disparaging you behind your back, call out the bad behavior and say, "Joe, what you are doing is disrespectful and not fostering a healthy collaborative work environment. I treat you with respect. You must treat me the same."

If your boss is piling on work with unrealistic deadlines or setting work expectations on short notice with due dates that cannot be met, review your workload with your boss and be honest about what is practical. If you are also working for others, ask them to join and help set realistic expectations.

In all of your communications, organize your thoughts, stand tall, and speak calmly and confidently.

Working for a superior who is a bully can be seriously detrimental, especially if they decide to impact your performance review negatively. Make sure to document the details of any troubling incidents, including keeping copies of inappropriate communications and noting any witnesses present to support your experiences. Ask those witnesses in advance if they will corroborate your account. For any work projects subject to your boss' performance reviews, collect accolades received from other colleagues or customers that will contradict his or her negative view.[40]

Working remotely presents additional challenges. It is not possible to walk into your superior's office to resolve any conflicts or disagreements. In a recent example, a young female associate at a consulting firm was updating her team via video conferencing call on a project she was asked to lead. Her superior kept interrupting her, apparently not satisfied with the order of her presentation, causing her to lose confidence in the content of her work, which she had spent long hours and nights developing. Flustered and humiliated, she conceded to sending her update to the group by email. No one on the conference call came to her rescue, not even the women.

How might she have responded? Take charge of your career and your person. Don't let anyone humiliate you in front of a group and say: "Respectfully, Mike, I would like to have just a few minutes to complete my update, which is one reason for our call today. I am available to talk offline later at your convenience if you have any issues or concerns about the update I am presenting or the project." Hopefully, your response will be a cue for others on the call to support your request. If you are a witness, do the same for the person making the presentation.

If, despite your efforts, your superior continues to interrupt or berate you, seek help after the call from a superior colleague with power and influence over the violator. He or she may be able to address your concerns with the appropriate results. Worst case, consider filing a complaint with HR, although this should be your last resort. This process can be mentally and physically daunting, and in the end, the issue may not be resolved in your favor.

➤ Dealing with a Narcissist

Narcissist behavior can be troubling and difficult to experience—especially in a work environment. Generally, a narcissist is deeply insecure and convincingly hides behind an armor of confidence and charm, even though they are very arrogant and have little empathy. Winning means everything to them, and they are constantly protecting themselves. They do not self-reflect, and they are not likely to ever change their behavior or mindset. To a narcissistic colleague or superior, you are typically considered an inconvenience, and they are not really interested in anything you have to say. As a leader, narcissists require excessive loyalty, praise, and adoration. They refuse to be challenged or questioned, are not interested in the opinions of others, seek positional power to ensure control, are extremely competitive, and take personal credit for the work of others or the team.

If you try to make a point during a meeting, a narcissist will respond by claiming that your statements are confusing and don't make sense. They will openly act like what you are saying is unimportant and rephrase your ideas into words or sentences that make your point sound confusing. They are also known to "gaslight," meaning they tell you about things you agreed to do, conversations you had, or things you said—which you never actually did, making it sound like you are crazy or incompetent. If things get heated, a narcissist turns the table on you and calls you too sensitive, emotional, hysterical, difficult, and unreasonable. Gaslighting can be a form of emotional abuse. It happens when someone—like a partner, parent, friend, or superior—challenges what you know is true and makes you question your beliefs and sanity.[41] Merriam-Webster's top definition for gaslighting is the "psychological manipulation of a person, usually over an extended period of time, that causes the victim to question the validity of their own thoughts, perception of reality, or memories and typically leads to confusion, loss of confidence and self-esteem, uncertainty of one's emotional or mental stability, and a dependency on the perpetrator."

Essentially, narcissists don't want you to have any value or respect in the conversation, ensuring that your point will not be heard. They will also criticize you for how you brought it up, your tone of voice, your timing or place of choice—poking at anything in order to dismantle your credibility.

They will do what they need to do to prevent you from getting to your point, unable to champion an opinion or idea that isn't their own.

Finally, a narcissist will say things to hurt you, strategically using insults to get you off your game. Their condition makes them highly skilled at finding and targeting your weaknesses. A narcissist also wants you to feel isolated by making you think you are off track, saying things like "no one else behaves this way," "no one thinks you are right," and "everyone thinks you are trouble."[42]

> ➢ How do you deal with a narcissist?

It's important to establish clear boundaries with narcissists at your workplace because they tend to push limits. You can do this by imposing guidelines for their behavior or communicating your expectations clearly and firmly. Document everything. Ensure you keep a record of any conversations or interactions you have with them in case they try to twist what you said and make a note of any inappropriate behavior or actions. This record will be enormously helpful if you eventually need to escalate the situation to management or HR. Include a witness to corroborate your claims, helping clarify any disagreement on what was said later. Make sure this witness understands your concerns about the violator. He or she can help set the record straight if needed.

Narcissists crave power and attention, so it's best to avoid getting into power struggles with them. Instead, control your own ego and need to win. Focus on maintaining your professionalism and staying calm.

Narcissists often act in ways that are hurtful and disrespectful to others. It's important to remember that their behavior is about them, not you. Don't take their behavior personally or let it affect your self-esteem. Don't let your own ego wanting to win, be right, or prove a point affect your personal growth. If you feel yourself getting emotional, detach yourself. By controlling your ego and emotions, you will appear more mature and professional.

If all else fails, inform HR of your concerns. If the situation is not resolved to your satisfaction, request to be transferred or moved to a different group or avoid interactions with the violator as much as possible.[43]

➤ Dealing with a Chauvinist

Merriam-Webster defines chauvinism as "an attitude of superiority towards people of the opposite sex," and today, it is said to go hand in hand with sexism.[44]

The most common example of a chauvinist is a man who considers females and their opinions trivial and inherently inferior to males, regardless of their job titles. In a work meeting, he will ask a female over a male to get coffee, make copies, make calls, set up meetings, and take notes—even though it is not part of her job description. He could easily ask his administrative assistant responsible for such tasks. The chauvinist will talk over a female in meetings, interrupt her desire to speak, or speak for her: "I think what Tammy is trying to say is..." He will also "mansplain," defined by Merriam-Webster as "explaining something to a woman in a condescending way that assumes she does not know the topic." He will often exclude her from difficult assignments or take away her ability to engage in tough negotiations by assuming she is not "cut out for the task"—all of which is harmful to her career progression. Although most people think chauvinism is more common within older generations, it is equally frequent among younger generations as well. During my experience as a young law partner, I remember one particular transaction where our clients were meeting in a conference room to resolve final open matters relating to the closing of a real estate loan transaction. The clients had never met personally, nor had the attorneys, so we decided to have a face-to-face meeting. When I walked into the conference room to introduce myself and start the meeting, one of the attorneys on the other side asked if I would please "fetch coffee and make some copies" for the group. He used a dismissive tone of voice, not considering that I might be the partner hosting the meeting. I smiled at him and directed my attention to the group to introduce myself as principal counsel for our client. Looking at him directly, I let the group know where they could find the bathrooms and that coffee and other refreshments had been placed in the adjacent room by my assistant for everyone's convenience. "Please help yourselves," I said. "We will be starting our meeting in about 10 minutes." Everyone chuckled, and the opposing counsel was embarrassed.

No matter how demeaning someone might be towards you when you first meet them, take the high road, be firm in your response, but set them straight—gently. First impressions and setting the tone are critical. If you don't have the opportunity to set the tone for a professional discussion because your opposing party insists on being difficult or rude, ask your client (or colleague or superior) to communicate your concerns with his or her counterpart. Throughout my career, there were a few instances where clients communicated that discussions would terminate if they didn't get their counsel and his disrespectful manner under control.

For example, in one case, opposing counsel seemed amenable and willing to consider compromises on conference calls. However, hours later, he would send me very hateful and disrespectful communications about my client and resolutions we were proposing to outstanding issues. It was an odd tactic apparently made to intimidate me. Did he not know I would forward these messages to our client and that his communications could potentially derail an important transaction? His own client ultimately fired him.

Another example involved a very heated discussion on a conference call with opposing counsel and his clients. Counsel was getting very frustrated, and his tone of voice became very disrespectful. When our clients refused to agree to a last-minute change in the terms for a property sale that had been finalized for weeks, the counsel exclaimed, "Maybe they should reconsider the bad advice they are getting from a woman!" It made our client furious, but before he could respond, I said, "Why don't we terminate this call until your counsel has collected himself and is willing to have a respectful conversation to resolve this unexpected new issue? You can reach us at this same number for the next hour if you are willing to continue this call. Thanks." Then I hung up the phone. The attorney never apologized; however, when we closed the transaction a few weeks later, his client pulled me aside and apologized for his attorney's behavior.

> How should you deal with a chauvinist?

Speak up and object. Gently, if possible. As noted, if a superior colleague asks you to "fetch coffee," "make a copy," "take notes," or anything else that does not fall within your job description, suggest: "Respectfully, let's ask your administrative assistant to do this so I don't have to miss any part of this meeting." At times, it's better to find a compromise and not appear disrespectful. If you offer a solution, he may think twice before he makes such a request next time. If there is no administrative assistant or subordinate, suggest that the participants take turns. If your superior insists that you handle his request in front of the group, talk to him about the issue after the meeting. However, try not to be accusatory or aggressive during this confrontation. Remind him you were hired (and are being paid) to work on projects for the group and not to do things that are more appropriate for other designated employees to handle. If he continues giving you inappropriate tasks, seek the help of a more senior colleague to help you resolve the issue. If you have no other options, file a complaint with HR.

If you are constantly interrupted by someone during a meeting, stop that person and say, "Respectfully, I am not finished," and continue your point. If a colleague thinks he must finish your thoughts in a demeaning fashion, interrupt him and say, "Respectfully, I can explain my own point, thank you!" and continue your point.

If a male colleague says something sexist, ask him if he would have said the same to a male colleague. Use humor to point out inappropriate behavior for a greater impact.

➤ Dealing with Sexual Harassment—Pick Your Battles

If you work in a male-dominated environment, you may be exposed to occasional male banter and teasing. This behavior is often meant to be funny or competitive and not as a personal insult. Pick your battles. Don't hesitate to dish it back if you feel comfortable, but try to stay out of the gutter and remain professional and calm when doing so.

➤ Draw a Hard Line of Respect

How you handle sexual harassment should depend on the nature of the harassment and the personality type of the abuser. Responding to a superior who is conditioning your job on a physical relationship with him is far more serious than taming a group of male colleagues who are commenting on a female colleague's body parts in your presence. Using a little humor in certain circumstances, especially where you are dealing with a group of violators, is likely to diffuse a defensive response to your admonition of the behavior. You are more likely to be viewed as looking out for the violator(s) if you offer positive feedback on how to behave better, which might foster trust and is less likely to create enemies at work.

If you find yourself exposed to inappropriate and sexist comments and behavior, don't hesitate to shut the violators down firmly but gently. I believe it is better not to put the men on the defensive in order to help them be more receptive to your feedback. Use a little humor in your response, at least the first time around. You could laugh and say gently, "Guys, seriously, did you just hear yourselves? Your comments are inappropriate! What would your mothers think?" If the behavior happens at work, you can even add, "If you are overheard, you could be subject to sexual harassment claims!"

If someone touches you inappropriately, remove the offender's hand, back away, or get up and create distance. Look the violator in the eye and tell him or her gently, "Hey! I am not available for touching!" If someone is standing too close to you or leaning over your shoulder and looking down at your cleavage, say, "Hey! Please back up. You are too close for comfort!" If the violator has done it before or is insistent, be more forceful: "Please stop touching me!" or "Please back up!" and "You are making me uncomfortable!" Stand up, if necessary, to emphasize your point. If you find yourself in a sticky situation with a superior who is conditioning a raise or promotion on inappropriate behavior, such as sex or an insistence that you join him in his hotel room to "discuss business" (and he does not take "no" for an answer), respond immediately. Say something like, "With all due respect, what you are suggesting does not fall within my job description. I am confident HR would want us to keep our work relationship professional!" If possible, use a light-hearted tone of voice to minimize a defensive reaction.

If, however, you are in the group and the banter and teasing are particularly offensive, or the behavior is directed at you, address the behavior using Plan A [Steps of Communication] noted in Chapter 3 of *Play Nice*. Your male colleagues will learn not to push you around.

Learn how to draw a firm line and create a boundary of respect. Use the playground rules from *Play Nice* to help with your communications: "Respect the playground and its players!" "Treat players how you want to be treated." "Respect the boundaries of your players!" "Inappropriate treatment of players is strictly prohibited!" Do it every single time you are exposed to sexual harassment. Be consistent. It is the best way to generate respect and trust from your colleagues and superiors.

Your colleagues will be more amenable to your admonishment and more likely to respect your position and learn from your guidance if you take action immediately, gently, and with a bit of humor. They'll be more relaxed around you, knowing if they act badly, you will put them in their place instead of running to HR. Remember that speaking up immediately is crucial to stop the behavior and feel comfortable in your work environment!

> ➢ Don't Be One of the Boys

Be careful. Being one of the boys has associated risks. You may think that staying silent or laughing at bad male behavior about women and their bodies may result in greater respect for you as a female colleague, make the men think you are tough, and get you invited to male "inner circle" activities such as meetings, lunches, and happy hours. However, know that you are complicit in the perpetration of this behavior if you tolerate inappropriate comments and do not take action to correct it. Who knows what these men are saying behind your back if they are comfortable speaking disrespectfully of women in your presence? Condoning their behavior will only encourage them to continue. Instead, consider interrupting bad behavior and educating your colleagues on the potential consequences of being overheard and turned in to HR. Help them understand why such behavior is demeaning and damaging to the health and well-being of their female colleagues. Surely, they would not want their mothers, sisters, or daughters to endure similar commentary. By humanizing the issue and making it something they can relate to, the perpetrators will be more likely to listen to your advice. Ask them to help and intervene when they see bad behavior themselves. Remind them that the perpetrator could be their brother, father, son, best friend, or work colleague, making it more critical to look out for them and discuss the importance of respect, consent, and boundaries.

> ➢ What if Your Customer or Client is the Harasser, Male or Female?

During a business meeting, your client turns the conversation to personal topics such as "Are you available?" or "I would love to get to know you better," or "Will you have drinks with me"? How do you handle client advances knowing that he is very important to the future growth of your company? If you do or say the wrong thing, your client could pull very important business!

First, you should not put up with any behavior you find offensive. We address this very important issue in *Play Nice*. Deal with the bad conduct on the spot. Be kind and light-hearted in your response. Let him know that you do not mix business with pleasure, that his business is important to you and your company, and that you are required to keep things professional. Be direct and clarify that his conduct is not appropriate, if necessary. "Hey, I am hearing some flirty comments from you, and they are making me uncomfortable. I am not permitted to mix business with pleasure, and I do not want to risk losing my job!"

Having dinner or drinks with a client after work is fine, especially if he is visiting from out of town. Just be sure to clarify your intentions prior to the encounter to avoid any misunderstandings. "Dinner or drinks after our meeting sounds great, but only if you agree it stays professional." Make sure he agrees in advance. If possible, take someone with you to encourage compliance.

Keep all communications professional, and don't share any information that may be too personal, including your home phone number. If your client instigates inappropriate behavior, discuss the conduct with a superior or male ally who can intervene on your behalf and help stop his overtures.

Not addressing the sexual harassment on the spot will only embolden continued bad conduct.[45]

➢ *Play Nice*—Playground Rules for Respect in the Workplace

Play Nice educates men and women on what constitutes sexual harassment using personal stories and real-world examples. It reviews the different types of violators, provides suggestions on how to handle them, explains why it is difficult for victims to report, and highlights the importance of bystander intervention. In *Play Nice*, we offer tools to help deal with bad behavior on the spot for victims and bystanders as the first step as an alternative to immediately reporting to HR to preserve jobs for both the victim and the violator. *Play Nice* also describes the progress of sexual harassment laws (or lack thereof) and the continued need for change, offering suggestions for companies and their HR departments to improve company culture and behavior.

Check out *Play Nice*, which is an important resource, and my related blogs at www.thesandboxseries.com. The blogs review plenty of recent news story examples of inappropriate behavior, the consequences endured, and how such situations might have been avoided. For example, the failures of Andrew Cuomo as the governor of New York (and how he might have handled the accusations against him differently) and the disastrous actions of his close circle of executives and HR department. Those failures only underscore the importance of educating all company employees, including managers, executives, and those in HR, on the devastating impacts sexual harassment and a toxic work environment can have on the mental and physical well-being of employees, the public reputation of a company, retention, and recruiting of employees and executives, and company profit and liability.

➢ Share Your Opinion—Gently

Don't be afraid to speak up and share your thoughts, especially if you are subject to or are witnessing bad behavior. Speak with confidence. Express your concerns in a non-threatening way to avoid putting the violator on the defensive. It never helps to start a fight, especially with someone senior. For example, if you'd like to contribute to a meeting and someone is disregarding your efforts to speak or interrupting you, stand up and let the group know you have something to say. "You have to be succinct, straightforward, and to the point. This action shows your own authority and expertise and tells others that you deserve to be respected and listened to."[46]

You have every right to contribute to the conversation and should not let male colleagues interrupt or control your ideas. Remember, being knowledgeable about the subject is empowering. "You are just as skilled, knowledgeable, and deserving. You were hired for a reason—your voice and your mind are valuable." Id.

Identify and Use Your Allies

Some of my best friends are men I met through work. If I faced gender discrimination, sexual harassment, or other untenable situations, my male buds would be the first to assist. According to a recent study, "women are more likely than men to experience backlash when advocating for gender equality or confronting sexism." "...others [may] be more receptive to men's messages of gender equality than messages delivered by women."[47]

Learning how to build alliances and foster support among male colleagues is important for creating a positive and inclusive work environment. Here are some strategies for building relationships with male colleagues:

Encourage open and honest communications to help bridge any gaps in understanding and to build empathy. You can do so through workshops or training sessions to educate about gender biases, stereotypes, and the importance of diversity and inclusion.

Use real-life examples for discussion and role play to illustrate good and bad behavior. If you see a teaching moment, take advantage and educate your colleagues on how to behave better.

Encourage male colleagues to mentor and sponsor their female counterparts, including regarding how to navigate company politics, the art of negotiations and deal-making, and how best to share successes.

Doing these can provide necessary guidance, support, and opportunities for career advancement.

Get to know your male colleagues and make friends. Turn them into your allies. You might need them someday to get you out of a difficult situation. According to reports, "Confrontations against sexism were seen as more legitimate when a man delivered the message than by a woman." [Id.]

Being the Manager or Supervisor

During my very first 'welcome to the law firm' meeting, a senior partner welcomed us new associates with a legendary quote from the 1973 movie classic, "The Paper Chase." Looming large over his audience, he said: In one of my favorite movies, Harvard Law School Professor Charles Kingsfield tells his students, "Look to your left, look to your right, one of you won't be here next year." While he emphasized, he was just kidding, we sensed the gravity of his words. He wanted us to know that the job would be demanding, and unfortunately, not all of us would endure.

Don't be like this senior partner. Statements like these can create a toxic, competitive work environment where self-preservation becomes a priority. Instead, focus on messages that encourage teamwork and collaboration.

As a leader, it is crucial to set a positive example for your team. You must embody the values of hard work, integrity, and respect that you expect from your employees. It is imperative to create a work environment that is free from bullying, discrimination, and harassment of any kind. Enforce a strict zero-tolerance policy from the top down to ensure a culture of respect and inclusivity within your organization.

Effective leaders are proactive in identifying and addressing potential issues before they escalate. Clear and open communication is key to building trust and fostering a positive work environment. By being transparent and honest in your interactions with your team, you create a sense of safety and support that encourages collaboration and productivity.

Encourage a culture of continuous learning and development within your team. Provide opportunities for professional growth and skill enhancement to help your employees reach their full potential. Emphasize the importance of teamwork and collaboration over individual achievements and recognize and celebrate the successes of your team to boost morale and motivation.

Lead by example when it comes to work-life balance and prioritize the well-being of your employees. Show empathy and support for their personal and professional challenges and promote a healthy work environment that values mental health and self-care. Remember that true success is rooted in happiness. Prioritize creating a positive and fulfilling work experience for your team.

Finally, stay informed about industry trends and best practices to ensure that you are leading your team effectively and staying ahead of the competition. By continuously learning and adapting to changes in your industry, you can position your team for success and drive innovation within your organization.

10

How Men Can Help Their Female Colleagues

Use Every Opportunity to Educate Your Male Counterparts About the Value Women Bring to the Table to Encourage Their Support:

➢ The Value of Gender Diversity

Plenty of recent studies and reports underscore the importance of gender diversity among leadership positions in the sandbox of the work environment.[1,2]

According to studies, a greater number of women in senior leadership and management positions was tied to stronger performances in organizations, including better financial performance, higher retention, better reputation, better problem-solving, and less conflict.[3]

A review of 2,400 companies conducted by Credit Suisse revealed a compelling attribute—companies that had at least one female member on the board yielded higher returns on equity and higher net income growth than organizations without a woman on the board.[4] According to Moody's Investors Service, a bond credit rating business, a higher proportion of women on boards is correlated with higher credit ratings. "We consider the presence of women on boards—and the diversity of opinion they bring—as being supportive of good corporate governance, which is positive for credit quality," the rating agency said.[5] "... [Yet] they still hold just 29% of seats." Id. The stocks of companies with low female board representation, in comparison, have underperformed. Id.

Further, women tend to perform better during a crisis than men, including the crisis of the COVID-19 pandemic. In general, leaders with strong interpersonal skills, "who emphasize employee development even when times are tough; who display honesty and integrity; and who are sensitive and understanding of the stress, anxiety, and frustration that people are feeling," are most valued during difficult times—traits that women more often exhibit.[6]

Another report found that when companies have inclusive policies and promote inclusive work cultures, they are more likely to achieve 63% increased profitability and productivity, 60% greater ability to attract and retain talent, 59% greater creativity and innovation, and improve the company's reputation by 58%.[7]

The leadership qualities exercised by women are critical to a company's success. Women are more likely to be better at overall organization and details, including developing, managing, and motivating teams, encouraging participation, communicating changes in direction, setting expectations, and assessing capabilities. Women are more likely to be emotionally connected, thus enabling them to motivate and inspire coworkers effectively.[8]

Men and women working together serve as valuable assets to one another, especially in a company environment. The variety of viewpoints, market insights, and ideas that arise when we collaborate with people of different genders, ethnicities, religions, races, and sexual orientations results in improved problem-solving and profitability. If your male colleagues still need proof of this, a Gallup study involving a hundred business units from two companies in the retail and hospitality industries found "that hiring a demographically diverse workforce can improve a company's financial performance."[9]

Diverse teams are also more likely to challenge one another's ideas, assumptions, and potential biases, causing members to reexamine facts and exercise greater scrutiny over their projects. This ultimately allows the team to be more objective, competitive, and innovative. A diverse team is less likely to make mistakes. As David Rock and Heidi Grant note, if you are a white male, "Hiring individuals who do not look, talk, or think like you can allow you to dodge the costly pitfalls of conformity, which discourages innovative thinking."[10]

Further, women make up a significant portion of the consumer base. Thus, having women in key positions in organizations helps provide relevant insights into the needs and preferences of this demographic.

In male-dominated environments, women bring enormous advantages, such as being gentle and calm when things get tense. In difficult negotiations, a woman's firm but gentle voice and friendly female gestures appear less threatening and help to resolve frustrating arguments. Women are also typically better team players as they are more concerned with relationships and mutual best interests than intimidation.[11]

I agree with Lisa Gates in her article for Forbes: "[Women] are much more naturally disposed than men to produce collaborative, durable agreements—meaning our agreements last, and don't induce lingering resentment. The only thing we lack is confidence and a bit of study in the exquisite tools and strategies of negotiation."[12]

Given all of the benefits of diversity, why are we not populating the sandbox with more women in leadership positions to change misogynist work cultures and improve profitability? Companies must take more action to increase gender diversity within their workforce and leadership.

In 2010, the "30% Club" was launched as a campaign in the United

Kingdom, with the goal of achieving a 30 percent population of women on FTSE-100 boards by 2020. Since its launch, the number of female directors has grown from 12.5 percent to 27.9 percent; however, companies' response to commit to the pledge has been slow—only fourteen CEOs of the UK's largest 100 publicly traded companies have pledged.[13] In June of 2014, the U.S. launched its 30% Club with a goal of achieving 30% female directors on S&P 100 boards by 2020.[14] As of March 2021, 30.47% of S&P 100 board directors are women, up from 20.2% at the launch of the U.S. Club chapter. <u>Id</u>. Similar chapters now exist in Australia, Brazil, Chile, Colombia, Ecuador, Eastern Africa, Hong Kong, Ireland, Italy, Japan, Malaysia, MENA, Mexico, Poland, Southern Africa, and Turkey.

The reason for the lack of promotion of women to leadership positions may not necessarily be related to issues regarding women's qualifications; rather, this lack of advancement may be the result of cultural beliefs and implicit biases against women held by company leaders. Implicit bias refers to when we have attitudes toward people or associate stereotypes with them without our conscious knowledge—preconceived, improper notions of gender and normative gender behavior.[15] Implicit bias includes a vast amount of discriminatory ideas, such as the belief that women are weak and thus unable to lead effectively, that women of a certain body type cannot be successful, or that women are not confident enough to ask for a promotion.[16]

These, though unconscious, unfair beliefs and biases may have a severely negative impact on the development of women in the workplace and the overall recognition of women as capable leaders.

In March 2015, the German parliament passed a new law requiring a thirty percent quota of women to be appointed to the nonexecutive supervisory boards of the country's largest companies and senior leadership positions in the public sector.[17]

Germany's new law followed a decade-long push by other governments in Western Europe. In 2008, Norway required listed companies to reserve at least 40% of their director seats for women or otherwise suffer dissolution. In the decade following, more than a dozen other countries set similar quotas at 30% to 40%, including Belgium, France, and Italy, subject to fines, dissolution, or being banned from paying existing directors if the new laws were violated.[18]

Germany, Spain and the Netherlands prefer soft-law quotas, with no sanctions. In Germany, companies have been slow to comply. The legislation does not appear to have penalties for noncompliance, and companies claim there is a lack of properly trained women for these positions.[19] As noted above, the UK and the U.S. preferred guidelines supported by the "30% Club."

Nonetheless, this type of legislation could be helpful in the United States. Nationally, only 27% of corporate boards have women serving on them, and only 17% of boards have minority members as of 2020.[20]

To date, there are only a few states that have laws requiring diversity among board members. California enacted a law in 2018 requiring public companies to diversify their boards.[21] However, this law and a similar California law requiring companies to add minorities and other underrepresented groups to their boards were litigated and struck down in 2021 as unconstitutional. Washington requires boards to have at least 25% of its members self-identify as women. Maryland, New York, and Illinois require boards to disclose their demographic makeup. Only a few others, Connecticut, Hawaii, Massachusetts, Michigan, New Jersey, and Oregon, are considering diversity disclosure requirements.[22]

There is, however, a new NASDAQ rule regarding diversity approved by the Securities and Exchange Commission (SEC). NASDAQ (National Association of Securities Dealers Automated Quotations) is an American stock market that handles electronic securities trading around the world. As of August 2022, corporations listed on the U.S. exchange are required to disclose board-level diversity statistics annually using a standardized template and explain why they do not have at least two diverse members serving on their board (one female director and one director who is an underrepresented minority or LGBTQ+). NASDAQ's Board Diversity Rule allows for a transition period for a company to achieve compliance and, additionally, a notice and cure period if there is a compliance failure.[23] If compliance is not cured after this period, a Staff Delisting Determination Letter will be issued.[24]

NASDAQ implemented its board diversity rule in order to promote diversity and inclusion among the companies listed on its exchange. NASDAQ relied on research and studies that demonstrate how diverse boards tend to lead to stronger corporate governance and business outcomes. For example, studies have found that companies with more diverse boards tend to have better financial performance, are more innovative, and have greater risk management. Additionally, diverse boards are more likely to represent and understand the perspectives and needs of diverse stakeholders, such as employees, customers, and communities. NASDAQ also considered input from stakeholders, including investors, public interest groups, and corporate leaders, to strengthen the development of its board diversity rule.

NASDAQ's new rule was litigated as unconstitutional, the challengers claiming that NASDAQ is "effectively [shaming] companies into appointing members of minority groups to their boards, while discriminating against other candidates."[25] The Fifth Circuit of the U.S. Court of Appeals upheld NASDAQ's new board diversity rule on October 18, 2023.[26]

Why Women Are Good Leaders

As women, we have attributes men do not have. We are gentle but firm, easier to work with, listen more than talk, build relationships and collaborate rather than compete, develop and motivate others through positive reinforcement, use relationships rather than muscles to reach goals, and solicit and incorporate the ideas of others before we make final decisions. We are more organized, better with subordinates, and straight to the point. When tensions run high, we are better at calming the group with statements like: "Why don't we take a break and regroup after we have a chance to evaluate where we stand."

Women are good managers because of their "mothering" instinct. This allows them to be more sensitive to issues that arise within working groups and better at resolving conflicts. Women are more empathetic and willing to work through problems for the betterment of the team. They are more patient and organized and pay better attention to details.

Dorothy Callihan, in her book *The Women in the Room*, gives a strong example of how women are unique in terms of their management and organizational skills. She describes their unique talent as a capability of tracking all of the pieces of a puzzle to make sure they fit and are adjusted as needed when issues arise. This ability is similar, she says, to how a mother organizes her family to get out of the house in the morning. Constant adjustments are necessary to make sure your project stays on track.[27] I agree with Dorothy 100%.

As an example, one of my specialties at my last law firm was handling loan transactions with franchised properties as security (such as 7-Eleven, Taco Bell, Wendy's, and Subway). At times, these loans involved hundreds of properties in many states around the country—requiring very intensive, hands-on organization for proper tracking and documentation of all the terms of the overall transaction. Each state's laws required careful consideration to ensure property title ownership and land survey issues were resolved so the properties could be properly pledged as security for the loans at closing. The loan documents for each of the states required modifications to satisfy local lien and recording considerations and to address any problems raised by lien searches and land surveys for each property. The more properties involved, the more details to be resolved. Any change to a transaction term would ripple through the sets of closing documents for each property. It could be a nightmare, especially if any of the transaction terms changed on the eve of closing.

My job was to make sure all issues were resolved, and all changes were properly made by the date and time of closing. Managing the closing process and all parties involved, including our local counsel issuing legal opinions, the title companies issuing title insurance policies, the land surveyors for each state, our clients, opposing counsel, and our hard-working staff (secretaries, paralegals, and attorneys), was a huge challenge. The time commitment and sacrifice our team made for each transaction was enormous. To this day, I am grateful for all the hard work and dedication of our various teams. I could not have achieved work success without them.

My point? My detailed organizational skills, my calm communication demeanor, and my patient management style were all assets to my then male superior. Thanks to my attention to detail, he did not have to worry over any final changes in the closing documents I carefully evaluated or the logistics of closing the transaction. All he had to do—and we used to laugh about it—was to show up when the matter was completed to pick up the check for legal fees we had earned at closing.

Unconscious Bias, Gender Discrimination, and Sexual Harassment

Encourage your male counterparts to educate themselves on the meaning of discrimination—what it looks like and how it affects women and society. Men should review their own biases and gendered habits, such as interrupting women or taking credit for their ideas, and try to make changes where necessary. They should be mindful of their own behavior. Are they passing women over for promotion because they have children? Do they believe women with children have too much on their plate and can't work overtime hours? Are they picking men over women for challenging projects because they generally believe women are not as capable as men? Are they challenging other men who engage in discriminatory behavior? Men will listen to men. Modeling positive workplace behavior is key.

This positive workplace behavior can be expressed by men in many ways, such as supporting female colleagues by listening to their experiences and concerns, speaking up for them if they are being discriminated against, and amplifying their voices—especially in front of other colleagues in meetings and work gatherings, is helpful in highlighting the value women bring to the working environment and their male counterparts. Ask your male colleagues to openly advocate for gender diversity and equality by encouraging your workplace to adopt policies and practices that support diversity, inclusion, and equality.[28]

Don't be a Bystander

After the launch of the "MeToo" movement in late 2017, the headlines of sexual harassment and abuse tumbled out at a rate almost impossible to keep up with. During this chaos, you may have been thinking: Who stood by and let this harassment and abuse go on unchecked?

There have been many horrific examples. Olympic doctor Larry Nassar victimized young athletes for years under the guise of conducting "special gynecological procedures"; school officials, coaches, and parents (allegedly) turned a blind eye. R&B legend R. Kelly reportedly mentally and physically abused young talent for his own personal sexual gain, keeping them captive in a cult-like environment and allegedly dictating every aspect of their lives.[29] According to a December 2017 Daily Beast article, this barely scratches the surface of R. Kelly's alleged litany of sexual misconduct and that of numerous others in the music industry, but such behavior appears to be widely accepted.[30]

What about actor and comedian Bill Cosby, well-known director Harvey Weinstein, opera singer Plácido Domingo, financier Jeffrey Epstein, actor Kevin Spacey and most recently Sean Diddy Combs? They have now been exposed for their assaults against women and men, many of whom were simply looking for a career opportunity, whether in movies, television, on stage, or otherwise.

Spacey's critical success was more important to producers and directors than the allegations and rumors that have long swirled around him.[31] On the set of "House of Cards," the crew was aware of his inappropriate conduct but did not report his behavior. The bystanders chose to tolerate Spacey's harassment—and even assault—of their coworkers rather than take action in order not to cause a scandal or potential backlash. This action begs the question, if the crew and its supervisors had taken the issue to upper management, would their complaints have fallen on deaf ears?

> ### What About in the Business World?

Even when companies have faced high financial costs due to destroyed reputations and extremely expensive settlements for sexual harassment claims, they are still slow to change their perceived culture of sexual harassment until they are forced to take action, whether publicly or financially. See Uber, Fox News (Roger Ailes; Bill O'Reilly), and CBS (Leslie Moonves) as examples. The reason is simple: companies are focused on current profitability and retaining high-contributing performers. In many cases, they "look the other way" and tolerate the behavior to preserve the alleged perpetrator's perceived value to the company. For more on this topic, please check out *Play Nice*.

If the secret of sexual misconduct in industries like show business or Wall Street isn't such a secret after all, and if people are now opening up about it more, then what should bystanders (both men and women) do about it? Admitting there's a problem isn't enough; men and women cannot simply stand by while their colleagues and peers are harassed, assaulted, and discriminated against. Men, particularly, can be a powerful force in the fight against gender discrimination and sexual harassment.

Ask yourself and your male colleagues: How many times have you been a witness, bystander, or enabler of bad behavior in the workplace? Maybe the behavior made you uncomfortable, and you did not want to get involved out of fear of ridicule or retaliation from your colleagues. You thought, surely someone else will report the behavior? Or maybe you were too scared to speak up for fear of being labeled a "troublemaker" and potentially affecting your job security? It takes a village to change the culture and prevalence of gender discrimination and sexual harassment in the sandbox of the workplace. This village includes you, whether executive or employee.

Walk your male colleagues through common examples:

If, as a bystander, you witness bad behavior—physical, verbal, or emotional—toward a woman or a man, you must say something immediately. If you are in a meeting (whether in person or online), speak up if you see a colleague not being heard and constantly interrupted or demeaned. It is okay to say, "Hold on, folks, Tammy has something to say. Please let her speak and finish her thoughts." or "Tammy is not here for your personal pleasure, and your comments are making all of us uncomfortable. She is here to help you with your product design (or transaction), and we do not need any inappropriate distractions. Let's keep this professional!"[32]

Let the other guys know their behaviors are inappropriate, disrespectful, and likely violating company policy. Men will listen to other men. If your company has ill-defined or no rules about workplace conduct, let the guys know they're probably violating laws that govern workplaces. Women can do the same. Using humor is helpful in these scenarios and is more likely to highlight the intended communication—as long as the offenders don't come away thinking it was all a big joke. It's crucial to communicate that although you might be using humor to diffuse and address the situation, it's actually a serious matter.

If the abuser is in a larger group and you don't want to "call him out" in public, try to remove the victim from the situation by pulling her or him from the group under the pretense of discussing an issue or showing them something and discuss the inappropriate behavior with the violator privately (especially if you are a peer or a subordinate). However, "calling him out" in front of the group will have more of an impact and will send your intended message not only to the offender but also to the group. Do this as a leader. Be bold!

Intervening safely and gently can be a powerful show of support for the recipient of the objectionable behavior. A simple comment might have an impact, such as "Hey, not cool!

Be respectful. You are violating company policy!" Men will listen to other men. Furthermore, speaking up and taking a stand will underscore your leadership qualities. By contrast, staying silent makes you complicit.

In any case, let the victim know she or he is not alone. Whether the victim decides to formally complain or not, tell her or him that you will be an ally—that may simply entail supporting the victim if she or he files a complaint or may involve you talking to the offender(s) again or to his/their superior. If the offender(s) continues the misbehavior, encourage the victim to go to HR and offer to accompany her or him. Follow the victim's lead on what she or he wants done.

Men should have open dialogues regularly with their female colleagues so they can get guidance on what misconduct they might be experiencing and how to help combat gender-based issues. These men should be willing to offer assistance if they learn the women are currently experiencing sexual harassment, gender discrimination, bullying, or other misconduct in the office.

Determine if your company has state-of-the-art training against sexual harassment and other bad behavior and whether violations are strictly enforced. If not, ask that changes for such training be promptly implemented. Encourage your company to reward upstanders and to handle behavior violations with transparency, respect, responsibility, and accountability.

Ask Your Male Colleague to Become an Advocate

Men can play a vital role in advancing gender diversity and inclusivity in workplaces by creating opportunities for their female colleagues. They can do this by advocating for them, exposing them to new projects, providing career guidance, and acknowledging their achievements. Additionally, men can help address unconscious biases and promote fair treatment for all women by providing constructive feedback and supporting women from diverse backgrounds.

Support Female-Friendly Policies for Promotion and Hiring into Leadership Roles

Finally, men are important for supporting female-friendly policies for promotion and hiring into leadership roles. Working to bring more women into leadership is an important way to advance the cultural change we need. That means instituting internal programs to identify and mentor prospective leaders early in their development and creating hiring practices that encourage employing a diverse workforce.

11

How Your Company Can Help Break the Glass Ceiling

Promoting Workplace Cultural Change

Fostering collaboration with male and female colleagues is crucial for driving workplace cultural change. Begin by convening meetings to collectively brainstorm ways to enhance workplace culture. Openly engage with management to address cultural shifts, fostering constructive dialogue. Once goals are set, establish committees to design and implement the necessary steps. This approach ensures effective implementation of discussed strategies.

Goals for Consideration to Help Effect Change:

> Transparency in Policies and Enforcement

Create transparency from the top down by implementing and regularly updating company policies against sexual harassment, bullying, discrimination, and retaliation in compliance with applicable laws (including procedures for reporting, investigating, and disciplinary action for any violations), and encourage employee feedback for any needed changes.

➤ 'Zero Tolerance' Directives

Set a tone of "zero tolerance" for even the highest, most respected level of employee (such as the President or CEO). Make it clear that the company will maintain and enforce, without exception, zero-tolerance against violations regardless of seniority. The company's most senior executive should frequently remind employees of the company's policies against sexual harassment, bullying, discrimination, and retaliation (including codes of conduct and organizational values), verbally and with regular memos, in the sternest and most forceful tone possible. Seek an immediate replacement if the senior spokesperson is also a violator.

➤ Anonymous Complaint System

Institute a secure complaint system (or other "safe" mechanism for reporting) for employees who wish to report anonymously. Any such complaints should be provided to HR and the board of directors (or a subcommittee of the board designated for such purposes).

➤ Unconscious Bias Training

Conduct regular unconscious bias training to foster awareness of hidden prejudices. Accomplishing this will help avoid discriminatory behavior and promote gender equality.

➤ Establish Mentoring and Educational Programs

Provide proper mentorship, sponsorship, and leadership training opportunities for women to give them the chance to succeed within the company, achieve supervisory roles, and earn executive positions.

- Develop More Female Leadership

Empower women in the workplace by promoting women into leadership and management roles. Establish programs to train accordingly.

- Foster Diversity Hiring and Promotion

Foster diversity and inclusion by populating hiring committees to include women. Develop hiring strategies that increase gender diversity without reducing or ignoring merit. Consider a quota of women. Set gender diversity inclusivity goals for upper management and hold management accountable for compliance.

- Provide Equal Opportunities for Work and Promotion

Provide women with equal work and opportunities for career advancement to showcase their skills and allow them to make a difference. Promote qualified women and minority representation on boards, panels, and leadership teams, including at client events, client pitches, and speaking engagements.

- Establish Female Friendly Recruiting Practices

Call for recruiting practices that encourage women to apply. For example, consider removing names and pictures from resumes and using numbered systems to help reduce subconscious gender bias, allowing for a fairer selection process. Or, implement recruitment campaigns that target women, especially in industries that are not typically associated with women, such as construction, utilities, and mining.

> Audit Hiring and Promotion Practices for Transparency and Equality

Companies can conduct an internal audit of their hiring and promotion processes to determine if women and minorities are being hired at entry level and into leadership roles at an equal rate as white men. Executing this can help to break the glass ceiling and ensure equal opportunities for career advancement. This endeavor will also help to identify and address retention issues for women and women of color. Transparency in the promotion process can eliminate bias and effectively break the glass ceiling.

> Audit Compensation for Transparency and Equality

Conduct a company-wide audit to determine compensation disparities among men and women holding similar positions. Once the audit is complete, determine where adjustments are needed to close any gender wage gaps and implement new structures in the future to promote equal pay. Consider adopting new policies to disclose salary ranges for jobs in postings and during interview processes, promoting complete transparency. With these efforts, you may find yourself looking at an expanded and improved talent pool.

> Create Flexible Work Environments

Promoting a flexible work environment is crucial for accommodating the diverse needs of employees. By offering options such as in-office, remote, or hybrid work structures, flexible hours or days, and part-time opportunities, organizations can empower their employees to find a work arrangement that suits their individual circumstances. This flexibility is particularly valuable for new parents or those who may need to care for family members or attend to personal obligations. Moreover, prioritizing work-life balance through these measures not only helps retain talented employees but also fosters a healthier and more productive workplace.

➢ Provide Generous Paid Parental Leave and Substantive Reintegration upon Return

Providing generous paid parental leave is an important benefit for the health and well-being of your employees. Consider a minimum of three to four months of paid leave with an additional extension of up to six months if needed. Additionally, upon their return, it is important to implement policies that support seamless reintegration into the workforce, ensuring continued opportunities for raises and promotions without any form of discrimination or reduction in pay.

➢ Provide Affordable and Accessible Childcare

For many parents, childcare is an important issue. One or both parental units may be forced to work a limited schedule in order to accommodate early pick-up requirements or stay home with their children if the employer does not provide affordable, quality, and conveniently accessible daycare. Hiring a full-time nanny is not necessarily affordable, especially for the younger parent pool. It can be expensive and difficult for nurses, doctors, lawyers, and other professionals with long or unpredictable hours to hire appropriate and trusted childcare. Providing affordable and convenient childcare to employees can alleviate distractions and worries, ultimately fostering more loyal and attentive employees.

Men and women need to drive toward gender equality in the workplace because it promotes fairness and provides women with the same opportunities as men—breaking down barriers that limit women's career progression. Achieving gender equality creates a diverse and inclusive work environment that fosters creativity and productivity and serves as an example for future generations of women, inspiring them to pursue their dreams and reach their full potential. Gender equality in the workplace will benefit not only women and their employers but also society as a whole.

Let's get to work cleaning up the sandbox to achieve this goal for future generations.

Conclusion

I hear white men complain more and more that they are being passed over for promotion because a woman or person of color was selected in their place. Some white men have added: "We just want the process to be equal and fair. It is not right that women and minorities are being given priority despite a lack of qualifications. Why am I being punished for being a white guy?"

Many employers have made diversity, equity, and inclusion a priority in hiring and promotion. Those efforts should be applauded. The goal is not to take opportunities away from white men but rather to level the playing field and allow employees of all genders, races, and ethnicities the opportunity to catch up and occupy positions traditionally held by white men.

Imagine a company's workforce as a pie. If people in one group (white men) have traditionally been getting a larger portion of the available opportunities (a bigger piece of the pie) for a longer period, the other group (women and minorities) will have received a smaller portion, which is inequitable and unfair. Striving for a better balance through implementing diversity, equity, and inclusion (DEI) practices and qualification training will likely, in the short term, deprive the traditionally dominant group (white men) of opportunities they were used to getting—even though, as a result, they are receiving their fair share. If, consequently, the business grows and becomes more successful (which is the goal of DEI), the number of opportunities available can be shared on a more equitable level among women, minorities, and white men. The "pie" will grow, and so will the opportunities for all—more fairly.

Note however, we need white men to be powerful allies, mentors, and sponsors for diverse talent. Women must "be mindful not to exclude them unintentionally. At the same time, however, white men should not exclude themselves. White men are a critical part of the mission to build a fairer and more inclusive world. And that right there is why we should care!"[1]

It takes determination, resilience, and a strong support system for women to work successfully in a male-dominated environment. Women must advocate for themselves, believe in their abilities, and seek out mentors who can provide proper guidance and support. Building strong relationships with male colleagues can also help break down gender-based barriers and create more opportunities for advancement. However, it is also important for organizations to recognize and address systemic biases in order to provide equal opportunities and support for all employees, regardless of gender and race. We need our male and female colleagues to help in that effort.

In addition, as women, we must make every effort to support our female colleagues. Whether it's a refusal to join in the tawdry banter about a female colleague, supporting a female colleague with her efforts to be heard, or publicly congratulating a woman on her achievements, standing up for other women both sets the standards of behavior for the entire organization and helps co-workers feel valued and supported.

The toxic culture of the work environment will only change once women stand up and own their power and voices with confidence.

Most importantly, more women need to be cultivated and trained by their male and female superiors to become leaders of the future, including in work environments not traditionally populated by women.

As an example, my older daughter, Samantha, was born a sports fanatic and had no trouble competing with any male in terms of sports knowledge. During her senior year in high school, we thought she might pursue a career as a sports announcer. When she started considering job options, Samantha announced that she would not put herself in that type of male-dominated environment by taking on such a position. Despite her passion for sports media, the job would not be worth how she would be treated as a woman in that profession. She had watched too many female sports journalists suffer discrimination. It made me sad, especially given her knowledge of sports, her outgoing personality, and her tough nature. At that time, I wished I could have told her sufficient improvements had been made to male-dominated fields to make them more comfortable for women. Deep down, I knew that was not yet the case. More work needed to be done. I had no doubt Samantha would have made her mark for success, but not without enduring discrimination for being a female sports reporter.

My sincere advice is, please, don't give up your dream job. Succeeding as a woman in a male-dominated work environment can be challenging, but it is entirely possible. This book has highlighted some of the key strategies and skills that women can use to break through the glass ceiling and achieve their goals. By developing a strong sense of self-awareness, building a supportive network, and mastering key leadership skills, women can overcome the barriers that stand in their way and thrive in any workplace. While there is still much progress needed to achieve true gender equality, with the right mindset and tools, women can succeed on their own terms and pave the way for future generations of women to do the same. But it's important to remember that success isn't just about merely fitting in. It's about bringing your unique perspectives and experiences to the table, challenging the status quo, and being an advocate for change. As more women enter male-dominated fields and break down barriers, we create a more diverse and inclusive workforce that benefits everyone.

So, don't be afraid to stand out and be different. Own your voice, embrace your uniqueness, and continue to develop the skills and traits that make you a valuable asset in any workplace. With determination, hard work, and a supportive network, you can achieve your goals and make a lasting impact in your industry.

Play Smart aims to bridge the gender barriers in the workplace and empower women to succeed on their own terms through professional excellence. Women and girls everywhere should never have to give up something they are passionate about "because they're a girl."

I hope *Play Smart* will help you in your journey to achieve success and make a difference at work.

Be Bold. You can do it!

Acknowledgements

I extend my deepest gratitude to my beloved family and friends for their unwavering support and engaging discussions on navigating challenges in male-dominated workplaces. A special thank you goes to JoRayne Tomlinson, whose friendship was instrumental in launching the first book of THE SANDBOX SERIES, *Play Nice*. To my husband, David, and my two daughters, Samantha and Nicole, your continued patience, love, and support means the world to me.

I am also grateful to my friends and former colleagues for sharing their personal experiences and advice. A heartfelt thanks to my male friends Willy Geiler and Jeff Blackman, part of our regular Friday lunch crew, for their valuable male perspectives. To my beta readers Rodney Acker, Mia Blackman, Kimberly Davis, Chitra Fein, Shauna King, Joel Ross, Katherine McCarthy and Suzy Bashore as well as my contributors, including Bright Social Agency and Cris Haest, my talented university student editor, Hope Brown, my daughter Nicole Kimichik, and my Fiverr editor, Isabella, your thoughtful comments and guidance were truly appreciated.

Lastly, I am forever beholden to my parents for instilling in me self-respect and courage, especially to my late mother, my hero warrior. I strive to follow in your footsteps always.

To all of you, I express my love and gratitude for your essential contributions to *Play Smart*.

Thank you.

Notes

Introduction

1. Kim Parker and Cary Funk, "Gender discrimination comes in many forms for today's working women," *Pew Research Center*, December 14, 2017, https://www.pewresearch.org/fact-tank/2017/12/14/gender-discrimination-comes-in-many-forms-for-todays-working-women/.
2. Matt Gonzales, "Workplace Discrimination Erodes Confidence in Women's Abilities," *SHRM*, March 8, 2022; https://www.shrm.org/resourcesandtools/hr-topics/behavioral-competencies/global-and-cultural-effectiveness/pages/workplace-discrimination-erodes-confidence-in-women.aspx.
3. Kim Parker and CaryFunk, "Gender discrimination comes in many forms for today's working women," *Pew Research Center*, December 14, 2017; https://www.pewresearch.org/fact-tank/2017/12/14/gender-discrimination-comes-in-many-forms-for-todays-working-women/.
4. "Law Firms Still Failing to Close the Gender Gap, September 23, 2021, *KS Branigan Law P.C.*, https://www.ksbraniganlaw.com/news/2021/9/23/law-firms-still-failing-to-close-the-gender-gap.
5. Marc Brodherson, Laura McGee, Mariana Pires dos Reis, "Women in law firms," October 2017, McKinsey & Company; https://www.mckinsey.com/~/media/mckinsey/featured%20insights/gender%20equality/women%20in%20law%20firms/women-in-law-firms-final-103017.ashx.
6. Bryan Robinson, Ph.D., "Gender Discrimination Is Still Alive and Well in the Workplace In 2021," February 15, 2021, https://www.forbes.com/sites/bryanrobinson/2021/02/15/gender-discrimination-is-still-alive-and-well-in-the-workplace-in-2021/?sh=3759297c7f1c.
7. "Anti-Harassment Requirements by State," by *Impactly*, updated April 4, 2021, https://www.getimpactly.com/resources/anti-harassment-policy-requirements-by-state.

8. Co-Chairs Chai R. Feldblum and Victoria A. Lipnic, "Select Task Force on the Study of Harassment in the Workplace," U.S. Equal Employment Opportunity Commission, June 2016; https://www.eeoc.gov/select-task-force-study-harassment-workplace.
9. As a reminder, the #MeToo movement is a social movement against sexual harassment and sexual assault. It started in 2006 when activist Tarana Burke used the phrase "Me Too" to raise awareness about the prevalence of sexual violence. The movement gained widespread attention in 2017 after actress Alyssa Milano encouraged women to share their experiences of sexual harassment and assault using the hashtag #MeToo on social media. The movement which continues through today, encourages survivors to share their experiences and aims to raise awareness about the prevalence of sexual misconduct in society. Over the last several years, it has led to the downfall of many influential individuals in various industries who have been accused of such behavior, and has sparked meaningful conversations about consent, power dynamics, and gender equality.
10. Brigitte Gawenda Kimichik, JD and JR Tomlinson *Play Nice – Playground Rules for Respect in the Workplace* (Dallas: Brown Books, 2019), https://www.thesandboxseries.com/playnice.
11. AllVoices Team, "The State of Workplace Harassment 2021," dated September 1, 2021, *AllVoices*; https://www.allvoices.co/blog/the-state-of-workplace-harassment-2021
12. Mehul Patel, "The Weight of Expectations – The 2020 State of Wage Inequality in the Workplace," *Hired*, https://hired.com/h/wage-inequality-report/2020/#intro.
13. "Do private women's clubs discriminate against men?" by Marilisaraccoglobal – *Global News*, updated March 29, 2018; https://globalnews.ca/news/4110963/private-women-clubs-gender-divide/.
14. Michael K. Hurst, "DBA WE LEAD: 5 Years of Empowering & Propelling Women Lawyers," June 2023, Dallas Bar Association/Head Notes
15. Skye Schooley, "Facing Gender Gap in the Workplace," *Business News Daily*, updated June 29, 2022; https://www.businessnewsdaily.com/4178-gender-gap-workplace.html.
16. "Equal Pay Counts: What Companies Can Do," *Lean IN*; https://leanin.org/what-companies-can-do-about-equal-pay#!
17. *"Play Nice—Playground Rules for Respect in the Workplace"* was published in May 2019. Please check out our book and website at https://www.thesandboxseries.com/playnice.

18. Brigitte Gawenda Kimichik and JR Tomlinson, *Play Nice – Playground Rules for Respect in the Workplace*, (Dallas: Brown Books Publishing Group, 2019); https://www.thesandboxseries.com/playnice.

Chapter 1

1. "Breaking the Glass Ceiling, Overcoming Invisible Barriers to Success," *MindTools* https://www.mindtools.com/pages/article/newCDV_71.htm.
2. Glass Ceiling," by Julia Kagan, Updated April 25, 2022, Investopedia.com, https://www.investopedia.com/terms/g/glass-ceiling.asp.
3. Anna Mok, Kimber Maderazzo, Lorraine Hariton, and Edie Fraser, "2021 Women CEOs in America: Changing the Face of Business Leadership," *Women Business Collaborative (WBC) with Ascend, C200, and Catalyst*. https://www.wbcollaborative.org/wp-content/uploads/2021/10/Women-CEOS-in-America_2021_1013-2.pdf.
4. Maggie Wooll, "Gender inequality in the workplace: The fight against bias," *BetterUp*, dated October 15, 2021, https://www.betterup.com/blog/gender-inequality-in-the-work-place.
5. Melanie Lockert, "Understanding what the glass ceiling is and how it affects women in the workplace," March 10, 2022, *Insider, Personal Finance* https://www.businessinsider.com/personal-finance/glass-ceiling#:~:text=The%20glass%20ceiling%20refers%20to,t%20represented%20in%20executive%20positions.
6. "Glass Ceiling," by Julia Kagan, Updated April 25, 2022, Investopedia.com, https://www.investopedia.com/terms/g/glass-ceiling.asp.
7. "Women in the Workplace – 2021," *McKinsey & Company, Lean IN*, https://womenintheworkplace.com.
8. Manuela Barreto, Ph.D., Michelle K. Ryan, Ph.D., and Michael T. Schmitt, Ph.D., "The Glass Ceiling in the 21st Century: Understanding Barriers to Gender Equality," American Psychological Association, dated January 2009, Chapter 1; *Researchgate*; https://www.researchgate.net/publication/265519989_The_Glass_Ceiling_in_the_21st_Century_Understanding_Barriers_to_Gender_Equality.
9. Beyond the glass ceiling: Why businesses need women at the top," *International Labour Organization*, September 2019, https://www.ilo.org/infostories/en-GB/Stories/Employment/beyond-the-glass-ceiling#introduction.

10. Susie Benitez, "Here's How To Work In A Male-Dominated Industry, According to Women who've done it," *Chill Times*; https://www.thechilltimes.com/heres-how-to-work-in-a-male-dominated-industry-according-to-women-whove-done-it/.
11. Beyond the glass ceiling: why businesses need women at the top," *International Labour Organization*, September 2019, https://www.ilo.org/infostories/en-GB/Stories/Employment/beyond-the-glass-ceiling#introduction.
12. Breaking the Glass Ceiling, Overcoming Invisible Barriers to Success," MindTools, https://www.mindtools.com/pages/article/newCDV_71.htm.
13. Avoiding Unconscious Bias at Work – Avoiding Accidental Discrimination," *MindTools*, https://www.mindtools.com/pages/article/avoiding-unconscious-bias.htm.
14. Jeffrey Fermin, "Reducing Unconscious Bias in Workplaces," *AllVoices*, June 5, 2023, https://www.allvoices.co/blog/reducing-unconscious-bias-in-workplaces.
15. Lindsey Galloway, "Why Men Get Promoted on What Could Be, While Women Still Have to Show Their Work," dated June 9, 2022, Chief, https://chief.com/articles/hiring-for-potential
16. Debra Cassens Weiss, "Showing anger can backfire for female lawyers, studies say; law prof suggests 'gender judo' response, abajournal.com, Aug 6, 2018, http://www.abajournal.com/news/article/showing_anger_in_the_courtroom_can_backfire_for_women_lawyers_study_suggest/.
17. Joanna L. Grossman, "Vice President Pence's "never dine alone with a woman" rule isn't honorable. It's probably illegal," *Vox*, Updated December 4, 2017, https://www.vox.com/the-big-idea/2017/3/31/15132730/pence-women-alone-rule-graham-discrimination.
18. Jeffrey Fermin, "Reducing Unconscious Bias in Workplaces," *AllVoices*, June 5, 2023, https://www.allvoices.co/blog/reducing-unconscious-bias-in-workplaces.
19. Why employers should have a sexual harassment policy," August 28, 2023, *Thompson Reuters*, https://legal.thomsonreuters.com/en/insights/articles/company-sexual-harassment-policy
20. Sydney Cone, Kate Gold, Atoyia Harris, and Sehreen Ladak, "Workplace Conduct Still Needs Improvement After #MeToo," Oct. 24, 2022, *Bloomberg Law*, https://news.bloomberglaw.com/daily-labor-report/workplace-conduct-still-needs-improvement-after-metoo.
21. Sexual Harassment in Our Nation's Workplaces," Office of Enterprise Data and Analytics (OEDA) Data Highlight No. 2., U.S. Equal Employment Opportunity

Notes

Commission (EEOC), Washington, DC, April 2022, https://www.eeoc.gov/data/sexual-harassment-our-nations-workplaces.

22. AllVoices Team, "The State of Workplace Harassment 2021," dated September 1, 2021, *AllVoices*; https://www.allvoices.co/blog/the-state-of-workplace-harassment-2021.

23. Nilanjana Dasgupta, "Seeing is believing: Exposure to counter-stereotypic women leaders and its effect on the malleability of automatic gender stereotyping," dated September 2004, Science Direct, Journal of Experimental Psychology, https://www.sciencedirect.com/science/article/abs/pii/S0022103104000253?via%3Dihub.

24. Understanding what the glass ceiling is and how it affects women in the workplace," by Melanie Lockert, March 10, 2022, *Insider, Personal Finance*, https://www.businessinsider.com/personal-finance/glass-ceiling#:~:text=The%20glass%20ceiling%20refers%20to,t%20represented%20in%20executive%20positions.

25. The Simple Truth about the Gender Pay Gap," AAUW, 2022, https://www.aauw.org/resources/research/simple-truth/.

26. Maggie Wooll, "Gender inequality in the workplace: The fight against bias," BetterUp, dated October 15, 2021, https://www.betterup.com/blog/gender-inequality-in-the-work-place.

27. Zara Abrams, "The Urgent Necessity for Paid Parental Leave," dated April 1, 2022, American Psychological Association; https://www.apa.org/monitor/2022/04/feature-parental-leave.

28. Chris Komar, Average Paid Maternity Leave in the US [2023], Feb. 7, 2023, Zippia; https://www.zippia.com/advice/average-paid-maternity-leave/#:~:text=As%20of%202020%2C%20Massachusetts%20offers,also%20has%20a%20similar%20polic.

29. Dana Tuszka, "Maternity Leave: A Working Mom's Dilemma," Stay at Home/Working Mothers, imperfectparent.com; https://www.imperfectparent.com/articles/maternity-leave-working-moms-dilemma/.

30. Zara Abrams, "The Urgent Necessity for Paid Parental Leave," dated April 1, 2022, American Psychological Association; https://www.apa.org/monitor/2022/04/feature-parental-leave.

31. The Reality of Maternity Leave on Women's Careers, *UMA*, https://beboldbeuma.com/the-reality-of-maternity-leave-on-womens-careers/.

32. Racial and Ethnic Disparities in Access To and Use of Paid Family and Medical Leave," Monthly Labor Review, 2019; https://www.bls.gov/opub/mlr/2019/article/racial-and-ethnic-disparities-in-access-to-and-use-of-paid-family-and-medical-leave.htm.

Chapter 3

1. Megyn Kelly, "*Settle For More.*" HarperCollins. New York. Copyright 2016. Page 211.
2. Groundbreaking and legendary New York Congressperson Shirley Chisholm made this inspirational statement back in the 1970s: *"If they don't give you a seat at the table, bring a folding chair."*
3. Jane Fang, "7 Ways to Excel in a Male-Dominated Workplace," dated June 18, 2020, themuse.com, https://www.themuse.com/advice/7-ways-to-excel-in-a-maledominated-workplace.
4. Katie Douthwaite Wolf, "Feeling Off Your Game? How to Bring it Up to Your Boss," The Muse, Updated June 19, 2020, https://www.themuse.com/advice/feeling-off-your-game-how-to-bring-it-up-to-your-boss.
5. Nicole Lindsay, "Taking Constructive Criticism like a Champ," *The Muse*, https://www.themuse.com/advice/taking-constructive-criticism-like-a-champ.
6. Jane Fang, "7 Ways to Excel in a Male-Dominated Workplace," Updated June 18, 2020, https://www.themuse.com/advice/7-ways-to-excel-in-a-maledominated-workplace.

Chapter 4

1. Jessica Taylor, "Seriously? 4 Ways to Handle "Other Duties as Assigned," updated June 19, 2020, *The Muse*, https://www.themuse.com/advice/seriously-4-ways-to-handle-other-duties-as-assigned.
2. Sarbanes Oxley Act (SOX) 18 U.S.C. §1514A; https://www.whistleblowers.gov/statutes/sox_amended.
3. Survival tips for working in a male-dominated profession," Work, February 20, 2020, *Feminista Journal,* https://feministajournal.com/survival-tips-for-working-in-a-male-dominated-professsion/.
4. Deciding what to wear to work isn't getting any easier for women, even as business dress codes relax," *the University of Reading*, March 16, 2023; https://research.reading.ac.uk/research-blog/deciding-what-to-wear-to-work-isnt-getting-any-easier-for-women-even-as-business-dress-codes-relax/.
5. "How women who dress business casual are perceived in the office," *Ladders/Office Life*, Updated July 16, 2021; https://www.theladders.com/career-advice/how-women-who-dress-business-casual-are-perceived-in-the-office.

6. What exactly is business attire?" *Ladders/How To*, February 18, 2020; https://www.theladders.com/career-advice/what-exactly-is-business-attire.
7. Joan C. Williams & Rachel Dempsey, *What Works for Women at Work – Four Patterns Working Women Need to Know*, (New York University Press, 2014), 83.
8. Jacob Passy, "One-third of office romances end in unemployment," *Marketwatch*, Updated Feb. 9, 2018; https://nypost.com/2018/02/08/one-third-of-office-romances-end-in-unemployment/#.
9. Kim Elsesser, "These 6 Surprising Romance Stats Should Be a Wake-Up Call for Organizations," *Forbes*, dated February 14, 2019, https://www.forbes.com/sites/kimelsesser/2019/02/14/these-6-surprising-office-romance-stats-should-be-a-wake-up-call-to-organizations/?sh=5d3029c923a2.
10. Cvetkovska, Ljubica, "25 Workplace Affairs Statistics for Business & Pleasure," *2Date4Love*, Dated January 4, 2021 https://2date4love.com/workplace-affairs-statistics/.
11. Cvetkovska, Ljubica, "25 Workplace Affairs Statistics for Business & Pleasure," *2Date4Love*, Dated January 4, 2021 https://2date4love.com/workplace-affairs-statistics/.
12. David Yaffe-Bellany, "McDonald's CEO Fired over a Relationship That's Becoming Taboo," *The New York Times*, dated November 4, 2019, https://www.nytimes.com/2019/11/04/business/mcdonalds-ceo-fired.html.
13. 13. Jason Abbruzzese, "Matt Lauer denies sexual assault allegation," dated October 9, 2019, *NBC News*, https://www.nbcnews.com/news/us-news/matt-lauer-denies-sexual-assault-allegation-n1064206.
14. Elian Peltier, "Plácido Domingo Withdraws from Tokyo Olympics Performances," dated November 8, 2019, *The New York Times*, https://www.nytimes.com/2019/11/08/arts/music/placido-domingo-tokyo-olympics.html
15. Amy Brittain, "MeToo movement," Updated June 2, 2024, Britannica, https://www.britannica.com/topic/Me-Too-movement
16. Kat Stoeffel, "How to Date (Responsibly) at Work," dated April 14, 2015, *Glamour*, https://www.glamour.com/story/dating-at-work-rules-for-dating-coworkers-tips-advice.

Chapter 5

1. Chandler MacLeod, "Overcoming Challenges In Male-Dominated Industries," dated in 2017, https://www.chandlermacleod.com/blog/2017/03/overcoming-challenges-in-male-dominated-industries.

2. Molly D. Shepard, Jane K. Stimmler, With Peter J. Dean, *breaking into the Boys' Club (Second Edition), The Complete Guide for Women To Get Ahead in Business*, (Taylor Trade Publishing, 2009), 110.
3. Lisa Rabasca Roepe, "10 Tips for Finding a Mentor—and Making the Relationship Count," dated December 7, 2020, *The Muse*, https://www.themuse.com/advice/how-to-find-a-mentor.
4. Jo Miller, "The People Who Can Open More Career Doors than You Ever Thought Possible," Updated June 19, 2020, *the Muse*, https://www.themuse.com/advice/the-people-who-can-open-more-career-doors-than-you-ever-thought-possible.
5. Elevate "How to Survive and Thrive In A Male-Dominated Workplace," March 15, 2021, *Forbes*, https://www.forbes.com/sites/ellevate/2021/03/15/how-to-survive-and-thrive-in-a-male-dominated-workplace/?sh=7673ae3c7d1b.
6. Emily McCrary-Ruiz-Esparaza, "The Boys' Club Culture Is More Common Than You May Think," *InHerSight*, June 25, 2019, https://www.inhersight.com/blog/research/boys-club-culture-more-common-you-may think#:~:text=In%20a%20survey%20of%201%2C500,abuse%20of%20women%20and%20minorities.
7. Liz Elting, "How to Navigate a Boys' Club Culture," dated July 27, 2018, *Forbes*, https://www.forbes.com/sites/lizelting/2018/07/27/how-to-navigate-a-boys-club-culture/?sh=27f965cb4025
8. Nelson, Audrey, "Women and the Good Ole Boys Club," March 28, 2017, *Psychology Today*, https://www.psychologytoday.com/us/blog/he-speaks-she-speaks/201703/women-and-the-good-ole-boys-club.
9. Lois P. Frankel, Ph.D., "Nice Girls Still Don't Get The Corner Office – Unconscious Mistakes Women Make That Sabotage Their Careers," Grand Central Publishing, 2014, Page 93.

Chapter 6

1. Brag! The Art of Tooting Your Own Horn without Blowing It," by Peggy Klaus, February 18, 2020, Business Know-How, Zen business, https://www.zenbusiness.com/blog/brag/.
2. Joe Miller, "3 Smart Ways to Upgrade Your Elevator Pitch," *The Muse*, dated June 19, 2020, https://www.themuse.com/advice/3-smart-ways-to-upgrade-your-elevator-pitch.
3. Grace Miller, "Referral Marketing Statistics: The power of word of mouth," Annex

Cloud; https://www.annexcloud.com/blog/42-referral-marketing-statistics-that-will-make-you-want-to-start-a-raf-program-tomorrow/.
4. Kristina Udice, "How to Survive as a Woman in a Male-Dominated Workplace," September 28, 2018, New York Girl, https://nygal.com/woman-in-male-dominated-workplace/.
5. Blake Morgan, "50 Stats That Prove the Value of Customer Experience," September 24, 2019, Forbes; https://www.forbes.com/sites/blakemorgan/2019/09/24/50-stats-that-prove-the-value-of-customer-experience/?sh=5733748d4ef2.
6. Surprising Social Media Statistics (2022)," dated January 4, 2022, *Apollo Technical*, https://www.apollotechnical.com/social-media-recruiting-statistics/.

Chapter 7

1. Heidi Lynne Kurter, "3 Effective Tips On How Women Can Be More Assertive In The Workplace," dated January 31, 2021, *Forbes*, https://www.forbes.com/sites/heidilynnekurter/2021/01/31/3-effective-tips-on-how-women-can-be-more-assertive-in-the-workplace/?utm_source=newsletter&utm_medium=email&utm_campaign=dailydozen&cdlcid=5e457eed5b099ce02f946740&sh=69af6df116f6.
2. Regina Borsellino, "How to Make Your Voice Heard in the Workplace (Especially as a Woman or Minority)," Updated October 14, 2021, *themuse.com*, https://www.themuse.com/advice/voice-heard-at-work-women-minorities.
3. Amanda Miller, "How to blow your own horn, without embarrassment or apology," dated March 12, 2020, *Ideas.Ted.Com*, https://ideas.ted.com/how-to-blow-your-own-horn-without-embarassment-or-apology/.
4. Ben Rogers, "Not in the same boat: Career progression in the pandemic," Qualtrics, Aug 26, 2020, https://www.qualtrics.com/blog/inequitable-effects-of-pandemic-on-careers/.
5. Joann S. Lublin, "How to Climb the Corporate Ladder While Working Remotely," *The Wall Street Journal*, Sept. 28, 2020, https://www.wsj.com/articles/how-to-climb-the-corporate-ladder-while-working-remotely-11601305764.
6. Kate Bratskeir, "Starting a New Job Remotely Can Be Scary—here's How to Impress Everyone Right Off the Bat," dated March 1, 2021, *The Muse*, https://www.themuse.com/advice/impress-boss-team-start-new-job-remotely.
7. Amanda Miller, "How to blow your own horn, without embarrassment or apology," dated March 12, 2020, Ideas.Ted.Com, https://ideas.ted.com/how-to-blow-your-own-horn-without-embarassment-or-apology/.

8. Bryan Robinson, Ph.D. Contributor, "7 Ways to Stand out So Your Employer Notices Your Good Work," dated February 6, 2021, https://www.forbes.com/sites/bryanrobinson/2021/02/06/7-ways-to-stand-out-so-your-employer-notices-your-good-work/?sh=1c6163326502.
9. Heilman, M.E., & Chen, J.J., "Same behavior, different consequences: Reactions to men's and women's altruistic citizenship behavior," Journal of Applied Psychology, 90(3), 431-441, (2005).
10. Regina Borsellino, "How to Make Your Voice Heard in the Workplace (Especially as a Woman or Minority)," Updated October 14, 2021, *themuse.com*, https://www.themuse.com/advice/voice-heard-at-work-women-minaorities.
11. Joanne Lipman, "Women are still not asking for pay rises. Here's why," dated April 12, 2018, *World Economic Forum*, https://www.weforum.org/agenda/2018/04/women-are-still-not-asking-for-pay-rises-here-s-why/.
12. Kelli Thompson, "Men Negotiate Their Salary 4x More Than Women – Here are 5 Ways You Can Level the Playing Field," dated April 18, 2022, Fairygodboss, https://fairygodboss.com/articles/men-negotiate-their-salary-4x-more-than-women–here-are-5-ways-you-can-level-the-playing-field?variant=variant1.
13. How to Negotiate the Salary You Deserve," dated June 11, 2021, St. Catherine University, Academics, Be in the Business of Breaking Barriers, https://www.stkate.edu/academics/women-in-leadership-degrees/women-negotiating-salary.
14. Mehul Patel, CEO, "The 2020 State of Wage Inequality in the Workplace," *Hired*, https://hired.com/h/wage-inequality-report/2020/#transparency-need.
15. Kelli Thompson, "Men Negotiate Their Salary 4x More Than Women – Here are 5 Ways You Can Level the Playing Field, "April 18, 2022, Fairygodboss, https://fairygodboss.com/articles/men-negotiate-their-salary-4x-more-than-women–here-are-5-ways-you-can-level-the-playing-field?variant=variant1.
16. Mehul Patel, CEO, "The 2020 State of Wage Inequality in the Workplace," *Hired*, https://hired.com/h/wage-inequality-report/2020/#transparency-need.
17. Amanda Barroso and Anna Brown, "Gender pay gap in U.S. held steady in 2020," dated May 25, 2021, *Pew Research Center*, https://www.pewresearch.org/fact-tank/2021/05/25/gender-pay-gap-facts/.
18. Lauren Collins, "How the BBC Women Are Working toward Equal Pay," *The New Yorker*, July 16, 2018, https://www.newyorker.com/magazine/2018/07/23/how-the-bbc-women-are-working-toward-equal-pay.
19. Jo Ann Jenkins, CEO, "Helping Women Retire Securely," *AARP.org/Bulletin*.

20. Lauren Collins, "How the BBC Women Are Working toward Equal Pay," *The New Yorker*, July 16, 2018, https://www.newyorker.com/magazine/2018/07/23/how-the-bbc-women-are-working-toward-equal-pay

21. Skye Schooley, "Facing the Gender Gap in the Workplace," dated January 14, 2022, *Business News Daily*, https://www.businessnewsdaily.com/4178-gender-gap-workplace.html.

22. Xaquin G.V., "Can we talk about the gender pay gap?" The Washington Post, October 26, 2017, https://www.washingtonpost.com/graphics/2017/business/women-pay-gap/?undefined=&wpisrc=nl_most&wpmm=1.

23. Jo Ann Jenkins, CEO, "Helping Women Retire Securely," *AARP.org/Bulletin*

24. Lauren Collins, "How the BBC Women Are Working toward Equal Pay," *The New Yorker*, July 16, 2018, https://www.newyorker.com/magazine/2018/07/23/how-the-bbc-women-are-working-toward-equal-pay.

25. Overview of BLS Statistics on Pay and Benefits," dated April 4, 2022, *U.S. Bureau of Labor Statistics*, https://www.bls.gov/bls/wages.htm.

26. Jennifer Liu, "How much do others make for the same job? Here's where employers are required by law to share salary ranges when hiring," dated January 12,2022, *CNBC*, https://www.cnbc.com/2022/01/12/states-and-cities-where-employers-must-share-salary-ranges-when-hiring.html.

27. Michele C. Spillman, "Pay Transparency: What It Is and Why You Should Care," Dallas Bar Association Headnotes, July 2023.

28. Aki Ito, "Employers are being forced to make salaries public – and that's good news for your paycheck," *Insider*, September 12,2021, https://www.businessinsider.com/pay-transparency-salary-range-disclosure-laws-colorado-employers-terrified.

29. KOAA Staff, "Since Colorado implemented pay transparency law, wages up 11.5%," updated October 21,2022, NewsChannelNashville, https://www.newschannel5.com/news/national/since-colorado-implemented-pay-transparency-law-wages-up-11-5.

30. France to fine companies if gender pay gap not erased, *Reuters*, March 7, 2018, https://www.reuters.com/article/us-france-women/france-to-fine-companies-if-gender-pay-gaps-not-erased-idUSKCN1GJ31U.

31. Lauren Collins, "How the BBC Women Are Working toward Equal Pay," *The New Yorker*, July 16, 2018, https://www.newyorker.com/magazine/2018/07/23/how-the-bbc-women-are-working-toward-equal-pay.

32. Anouare Abdou, "3 Things You Need To Know Before Discussing Your Salary Expectations in an Interview," February 22, 2022, *Fairygodboss*, https://

fairygodboss.com/articles/3-things-you-need-to-know-before-discussing-your-salary-expectations-in-an-interview.

33. Dae Cason and Maria McCallen, "How to Ask for a Raise at Work and Negotiate Your Salary," *theSkimm*,' dated January 1, 2019; https://www.theskimm.com/money/negotiate-salary.

34. How to Negotiate the Salary You Deserve," St. Catherine University, Academics, Be in the Business of Breaking Barriers, dated June 11, 2021; https://www.stkate.edu/academics/women-in-leadership-degrees/women-negotiating-salary.

35. Kelli Thompson, "Men Negotiate Their Salary 4x More Than Women – Here are 5 Ways You Can Level the Playing Field," April 18, 2022, Fairygodboss, https://fairygodboss.com/articles/men-negotiate-their-salary-4x-more-than-women–here-are-5-ways-you-can-level-the-playing-field?variant=variant1.

36. Regina Borsellino, "3 Strategies for Answering "What Are Your Salary Expectations?" in an Interview," dated January 24, 2022, *The Muse*, https://www.themuse.com/advice/what-are-your-salary-expectations-interview-question-answer-examples.

37. How to Ask for a Raise and Get It," Payscale, https://www.payscale.com/research-and-insights/how-to-ask-for-a-raise/.

38. Mehul Patel, "The Weight of Expectations – The 2020 State of Wage Inequality in the Workplace," *Hired*, https://hired.com/h/wage-inequality-report/2020/#intro.

Chapter 8

1. Jeffrey Bunn, "5 Reasons to Exercise before Work," Freshgigs; https://www.freshgigs.ca/blog/5-reasons-to-exercise-before-work/

2. Ben Snider-McGrath, "Survey finds that morning exercise can boost creativity, productivity at work," Running, September 10, 2020; https://runningmagazine.ca/the-scene/survey-finds-that-morning-exercise-can-boost-creativity-productivity-at-work/.

3. Elizabeth Perry, "Breaks for breakthroughs: The importance of taking breaks during the workday," BetterUp, August 23, 2022; https://www.betterup.com/blog/the-importance-of-taking-breaks#:~:text=Here%27s%20what%20they%20found%3A,refreshed%20their%20perspective%20on%20work.

4. Terri Williams, "Report: Only 6% of U.S. companies offer comprehensive childcare benefits," dated February 27, 2020, *MultiBriefs – Exclusive*; https://exclusive.multibriefs.com/content/report-only-6-of-us-companies-offer-comprehensive-child-care-benefits/education.

5. Bringing transparency to the private sector," Skimm Impact, https://www.theskimm.com/paid-family-leave-benefits
6. Sara Gaynes Levy, "We Need to Talk About Mental Health at Work, *Glamour*, March 28, 2018, https://www.glamour.com/story/mental-health-at-work
7. Americans with Disabilities Act of 1990, 42 U.S.C. § 12101 (1990)
8. Liz Hilton Segel and Kana Enomoto," 5 Ways Employers Can Support Women's Mental Health," dated June 11, 2012; *Harvard Business Review*; https://hbr.org/2021/06/5-ways-employers-can-support-womens-mental-health

Chapter 9

1. Olga Khazan, "Why Do Women Bully Each Other at Work?" Updated August 3, 2017, *the Atlantic*, https://www.theatlantic.com/magazine/archive/2017/09/the-queen-bee-in-the-corner-office/534213/.
2. Why Women Prefer Male Bosses," January 9, 2019, *The Atlantic*, https://www.theatlantic.com/video/index/549818/women-prefer-male-bosses/.
3. Pamela Marrone, "Nine Tips for Succeeding as a Woman in a Male-Dominated World," *Ellevate*, https://www.ellevatenetwork.com/articles/9048-nine-tips-for-succeeding-as-a-woman-in-a-male-dominated-world.
4. Matthew Lavietes, "COVID-19 could wipe out gains in equality for women at work – U.N.," World Economic Forum, dated July 6, 2020, https://www.weforum.org/agenda/2020/07/u-n-warns-covid-19-could-wipe-out-gains-in-equality-for-women-at-work/
5. Karen Ho, "September was a disaster for women," *Quartz*, dated October 2, 2020, https://qz.com/1912491/us-jobs-report-for-september-shows-865000-fewer-working-women/.
6. Matt Gonzalez, "Nearly 2 Million Fewer Women in Labor Force," *SHRM*, February 17, 2022, https://www.shrm.org/resourcesandtools/hr-topics/behavioral-competencies/global-and-cultural-effectiveness/pages/over-1-million-fewer-women-in-labor-force.aspx.
7. Megan Brenan, "Working Moms Get Little Reprieve from Household Demands," *Gallup*, March 5, 2020, https://news.gallup.com/poll/286739/working-moms-little-reprieve-household-demands.aspx
8. Kristi Pahr, "Study Shows Moms Who Earn More Than Dads Do More of the Housework," Fatherly, April 2022, https://www.fatherly.com/news/study-shows-that-moms-who-earn-more-than-dads-do-more-of-the-housework.

9. Anneken Tappe, "Working mothers are quitting to take care of their kids, and the US job market may never be the same," Updated August 19, 2020, CNN Business, https://www.cnn.com/2020/08/19/economy/women-quitting-work-child-care/index.html.

10. Matt Gonzalez, "Nearly 2 Million Fewer Women in Labor Force," *SHRM*, February 17, 2022, https://www.shrm.org/resourcesandtools/hr-topics/behavioral-competencies/global-and-cultural-effectiveness/pages/over-1-million-fewer-women-in-labor-force.aspx.

11. Sheryl Sandberg and Rachel Thomas, "The coronavirus pandemic is creating a 'double double shift' for women. Employers must help," dated May 7, 2020, *Fortune*, https://fortune.com/2020/05/07/coronavirus-women-sheryl-sandberg-lean-in-employers-covid-19/.

12. Felicity Hannah, "How Covid is hurting women's financial health," *Independent*, dated June 23, 2020, https://www.independent.co.uk/money/spend-save/coronavirus-women-finances-pay-gap-jobs-furloughed-retirement-household-children-school-a9580671.html.

13. Jo Ann Jenkins, CEO, "Helping Women Retire Securely," *AARP.org/Bulletin*.

14. Craig L, Churchill B (2021) Dual-earner parent couples' work and care during COVID-19. *Gend Work Organ* 28, 66–79

15. Xue B, McMunn A (2021) Gender differences in unpaid care work and psychological distress in the U.K. COVID-19 lockdown. *PLoS One* 16, e0247959.

16. Platts K., Breckon J., and Marshall E (2022) Enforced home-working under lockdown and its impact on employee wellbeing: a cross-sectional study. *BMC Public Health* 22, 199

17. Gender Difference in working from home and psychological distress – A national survey of U.S. employees during the COVID-19 pandemic," Industrial Health, dated May 16, 2022; https://www.ncbi.nlm.nih.gov/pmc/articles/PMC9453567/.

18. Sheryl Sandberg, "Companies and Women Are at a Crossroads," *The Wall Street Journal*, dated September 30, 2020, https://www.wsj.com/articles/sheryl-sandberg-companies-and-women-are-at-a-crossroads-11601434004?mod=itp_wsj&mod=&mod=djemITP_h

19. Shelly J. Correll, Stephen Benard, and In Paik, "Getting a Job: Is There a Motherhood Penalty?" American Journal of Sociology 112, no.5 (2007); 1297-1339.

20. David Rock and Heidi Grant, "Why Diverse Teams Are Smarter," Harvard Business Review, dated November 4, 2016, httpbs://hbr.org/2016/11/why-diverse-teams-are-smarter?referral=03759&cm_vc=rr_item_page.bottom.

21. Associative Press, "COVID-19 and its impact on women at work," Shoosmith, https://www.shoosmiths.co.uk/insights/articles/covid19/covid-19-and-its-impact-on-women-at-work.
22. Lauren Weber and Vanessa Fuhrmans, "How the Coronavirus Crisis Threatens to Set Back Women's Careers," The Wall Street Journal, dated September 30, 2020, https://www.wsj.com/articles/how-the-coronavirus-crisis-threatens-to-set-back-womens-careers-11601438460.
23. Brigitte Kimichik, "Working From Home–Yes, There Is A Silver Lining," May 25, 2020, https://www.thesandboxseries.com/working-from-home-yes-there-is-a-silver-lining.
24. Brigitte Kimichik, "Working From Home–Turning Obstacles into Positives," May 20, 2020, https://www.thesandboxseries.com/working-from-home-turning-obstacles-in-to-positives.
25. Brigitte Kimichik, "Working at Home With Your Partner? Our Favorite Advice," https://www.thesandboxseries.com/working-at-home-with-your-partner-our-favorite-advice.
26. David G. Smith and W. Brad Johnson, "3 Ways to Advance Gender Equity as We Return to the Office," *Harvard Business Review*, dated June 11, 2020, https://hbr.org/2020/06/3-ways-to-advance-gender-equity-as-we-return-to-the-office.
27. Harriet Torry, "Women Embrace Flexible Working, but Economists Say It Could Hinder Their Careers," *The Wall Street Journal*, March 13, 2022, https://www.wsj.com/articles/women-embrace-flexible-working-but-economists-say-it-could-hinder-their-careers-11647180001.
28. Dr. Shawn Andrews, "Why Women Don't Always Support Other Women," dated January 21, 2020, *Forbes*, https://www.forbes.com/sites/forbescoachescouncil/2020/01/21/why-women-dont-always-support-other-women/?sh=17bd3d8f3b05.
29. Why Women Prefer Male Bosses," January 9, 2019, *The Atlantic*, https://www.theatlantic.com/video/index/549818/women-prefer-male-bosses/.
30. Why Do Women Bully Each Other at Work?" by Olga Khazan, Updated August 3, 2017, *the Atlantic*, https://www.theatlantic.com/magazine/archive/2017/09/the-queen-bee-in-the-corner-office/534213/.
31. Amy Tennery, "The Real Reason Women Don't Help Other Women at Work," dated May 11, 2012, Time, Career Strategies, https://business.time.com/2012/05/11/the-real-reason-women-dont-help-other-women-at-work/.

32. Marijana Stojanovic, Toxic work environment: how to recognize the red flags and what to do," dated April 28, 2022, *Clockify*, https://clockify.me/blog/business/toxic-work-environment/.
33. 10 Signs you're in a Toxic Work Environment, by *Career Contessa*, https://www.careercontessa.com/advice/toxic-work-environment/.
34. Kaelyn Barron, "How to Set Boundaries: Healthy Lines to Draw at Work and Home," *TCKpublishing.com*, https://www.tckpublishing.com/how-to-set-boundaries/.
35. Marguerite Ward, "5 warning signs you're in a toxic workplace, and what to do about it before it ruins your personal life," updated August 3, 2021, *Insider*, https://www.businessinsider.com/how-to-know-if-your-job-is-a-toxic-workplace-psychologists.
36. The Pink Ghetto, Above the Law, https://abovethelaw.com/tag/the-pink-ghetto/.
37. Meredith Mandell and Hilary Rosenthal, "Proskauer, a law firm known for handling high-profile sex harassment cases, is accused itself." NBC News, published online May 15, 2018; https://www.nbcnews.com/news/us-news/proskauer-law-firm-known-handling-high-profile-sex-harassment-cases-n874411.
38. "A Current Glance at Women in the Law." American Bar Association. Commission on Women in the Profession, Published January 2018, https://www.pbi.org/docs/default-source/default-document-library/10569_a-current-glance-at-women-in-the-law-jan-2018-(1).pdf.
39. Dr. Gary Namie, "2021 WBI U.S. Workplace Bullying Survey, dated 2022, *Workplace Bullying Institute*, https://workplacebullying.org/2021-wbi-survey/.
40. Stav Ziv, "Don't Let Workplace Bullies Win-Here's How to Spot them and Stop them," *The Muse*, January 26, 2022, https://www.themuse.com/advice/how-to-deal-with-workplace-bullies.
41. Smitha Bhandari, MD, "Gaslighting: What it is and how to stop it," dated August 3, 2022, *WebMD*, https://www.webmd.com/mental-health/ss/slideshow-gaslighting-what-it-is-and-how-to-stop-it.
42. A narcissist also wants you to feel isolated by making you think you are off track, saying things like "no one else behaves this way," "no one thinks you are right," and "everyone thinks you are trouble." https://fb.watch/v/1lfBmD-g-/
43. Nicole Lipkin, "How to Protect Yourself When Working with a Narcissist," dated November 17, 2020, Forbes, https://www.forbes.com/sites/nicolelipkin/2020/11/17/how-to-protect-yourself-when-working-with-a-narcissist/?sh=3f1273fa5ef5.
44. Taylor Tobin, "A Career Woman's Guide to Chauvinism," dated October 2, 2018, Fairygodboss, https://fairygodboss.com/career-topics/male-chauvinists.

45. Michele McGovern, "What to do when a customer hits on you," dated March 19, 2018, Insight/Communications, https://www.customerexperienceinsight.com/what-to-do-when-a-customer-hits-on-you/.
46. Kristina Udice, "How to Survive as a Woman in a Male-Dominated Workplace," New York Gal; https://nygal.com/woman-in-male-dominated-workplace.
47. Charlotte E. Moser, "Male Allies at Work: Gender-Quality Supportive Men Reduce Negative Underrepresentation Effects among Women," Sage Journals, August 9, 2021, https://journals.sagepub.com/doi/10.1177/19485506211033748.

Chapter 10

1. The Boardlist, "5 reasons why having women in leadership benefits your entire company," *Medium.com*, September 5, 2016, https://medium.com/@theBoardlist/5-reasons-why-having-women-in-leadership-benefits-your-entire-company-labor-day-2016-a3e46162a7a0.
2. Marcus Noland and Tyler Moran, "Study: Firms with More Women in the C-Suite Are More Profitable," *Harvard Business Review*, February 8, 2016, https://hbr.org/2016/02/study-firms-with-more-women-in-the-c-suite-are-more-profitable.
3. Catalyst Information Center, "Why Diversity Matters," July 2013, http://www.catalyst.org/system/files/why_diversity_matters_catalyst_0.pdf.
4. David Rock and Heidi Grant, "Why Diverse Teams Are Smarter, *Harvard Business Review*, November 4, 2016, https://hbr.org/2016/11/why-diverse-teams-are-smarter?referral=03759&cm_vc=rr_item_page.botto.
5. Yun Li, "More women in the boardroom could drive higher credit ratings and stock returns for firms—they still hold just 29% of seats," *CNBC – Equity and Opportunity*, March 11, 2022, https://www.cnbc.com/2022/03/11/women-gain-ground-in-the-boardroom-holding-29percent-of-director-seats-in-2022.html.
6. Jack Zenger and Joseph Folkman, "Research: Women Are Better Leaders during a Crisis," *Harvard Business Review*, December 30, 2020, https://hbr.org/2020/12/research-women-are-better-leaders-during-a-crisis?utm_medium=social&utm_campaign=hbr&utm_source=linkedin&tpcc=orgsocial_edit.
7. Beyond the glass ceiling: Why businesses need women at the top," *International Labour Organization*, September 2019, https://www.ilo.org/infostories/en-GB/Stories/Employment/beyond-the-glass-ceiling#introduction.

8. Georges Desvaux and Sandrine Devillard, "Women Matter 2: Female leadership, a Competitive Edge for the Future," McKinsey & Company, May 6, 2018, https://www.mckinsey.com/~/media/McKinsey/Business%20Functions/Organization/Our%20Insights/Women%20matter/Women_matter_oct2008_english.ashx
9. Sangeeta Bharadwaj Badal, "The Business Benefits of Gender Diversity," *Gallup Business Journal*, January 20, 2014, http://news.gallup.com/businessjournal/166220/business-benefits-gender-diversity.aspx.
10. David Rock and Heidi Grant, "Why Diverse Teams Are Smarter," *Harvard Business Review*, November 4, 2016, https://hbr.org/2016/11/why-diverse-teams-are-smarter.
11. Katie Shonk, "Challenges Facing Women Negotiators: The Impact of Leadership Styles on Strategic Decisions," Program on Negotiation (blog), *Harvard Law School*, February 18, 2018, https://www.pon.harvard.edu/daily/leadership-skills-daily/women-and-negotiation-leveling-the-playing-field/.
12. Lisa Gates, "Why Women Are Better Negotiators than Men," *Forbes*, August 5, 2011. https://www.forbes.com/sites/shenegotiates/2011/08/05/why-women-are-better-negotiators-than-men/#1789e0d57f72.
13. John Detrixhe, "CEOs of Big UK Companies Are Reluctant to Commit to Promoting Women to Top Roles," *Quartz at Work*, January 9, 2018. https://work.qz.com/1175275/30-club-only-14-of-the-uks-ftse-100-companies-have-committed-to-promoting-women-to-30-of-top-roles/.
14. About U.S. 30% Club," 30% + Club – A Path to Parity; https://30percentclub.org/chapters/usa/
15. Wendi S. Lazar, Terese M. Connolly, and Gregory Chiarello, *Zero Tolerance; Best Practices for Combating Sex-Based Harassment in the Legal Profession* (American Bar Association, 2018); "Implicit Bias Explained," Perception Institute, https://perception.org/research/implicit-bias/.
16. Lucy Shea, "Why Aren't There More Women in Leadership Positions?" Genbiz, October 23, 2017, https://genbiz.com/arent-women-leadership-positions
17. Alanna Petroff, "Germany's New 30% Rule for Women on Boards," CNNMoney, March 8, 2015, http://money.cnn.com/2015/03/06/news/women-boards-germany-30/index.html.
18. Ten years on from Norway's quota for women on corporate boards," The Economist, Business, February 17, 2018 https://www.economist.com/business/2018/02/17/ten-years-on-from-norways-quota-for-women-on-corporate-boards#.
19. Renuka Rayasam, "Why Germany's New Quota for Women on Boards

Looks like a Bust," *Fortune*, March 11, 2016, http://fortune.com/2016/03/11/germany-board-quota-women/.

20. Aracely Munoz, Nasdaq's new rule on board diversity is a good first step, not a gold standard," *Fortune*, August 8, 2022, https://fortune.com/2022/08/08/nasdaq-new-rule-board-diversity-sec-aracely-munoz/.

21. California Senate Bill No. 826, Chapter 954, published 10/01/2018, https://urlisolation.com/browser.

22. Will More States Set Board Diversity Mandates?" *LexisNexis*, January 13, 2022, https://www.lexisnexis.com/community/insights/legal/capitol-journal/b/state-net/posts/will-more-states-set-board-diversity-mandates.

23. NASDAQ's Board Diversity Rule: What Companies Should Know," NASDAQ, updated February 28, 2023; https://urlisolation.com/browser If compliance is not cured after this period, a Staff Delisting Determination Letter will be issued. Albert Lung & Emily Drazan Chapman, "Nasdaq Diversity Rules: A Quick Guide," *Morgan Lewis*, September 21, 2021, https://www.morganlewis.com/pubs/2021/09/nasdaq-diversity-rules-a-quick-guide.

24. Albert Lung & Emily Drazan Chapman, "Nasdaq Diversity Rules: A Quick Guide," *Morgan Lewis*, September 21, 2021, https://www.morganlewis.com/pubs/2021/09/nasdaq-diversity-rules-a-quick-guide

25. Alexander Osipovich, "Nasdaq Board-Diversity Rule Takes Center Stage in Court Battle," *Wall Street Journal*, August 29, 2022, https://www.wsj.com/articles/nasdaq-board-diversity-rule-takes-center-stage-in-court-battle-11661799731.

26. Donald Kalfen, "Federal Appeals Court Upholds Nasdaq Board Diversity Rule," Meridian, November 9, 2023; https://www.meridiancp.com/insights/federal-appeals-court-upholds-nasdaq-board-diversity-rule/#:~:text=Nasdaq%27s%20board%20diversity%20rule%20survives,this%20requirement%20is%20not%20met.

27. Dorothy Callihan, *the Women in the Room*, "How I Realized the Unique Value of Women in the Male-Dominated Workplace," 2017.

28. EJ Peters, "Feminism in the Workplace Supports Everyone," *elevate*, https://www.ellevatenetwork.com/articles/10992-feminism-in-the-workplace-supports-everyone.

29. Janice Williams, "R. Kelly's Alleged Victims: A Timeline of Sexual Misconduct Allegations against the R&B Singer," October 24, 2017, *Culture*, https://www.newsweek.com/r-kelly-sexual-accusations-abuse-691776.

30. Marlow Stern, "Why Has the Public Forgiven R. Kelly for His Sordid, Predatory Past?" July 11, 2017 https://www.thedailybeast.com/why-has-the-public-forgiven-r-kelly-for-his-sordid-predatory-past.
31. E. Alex Jung, "Man Comes Forward to Describe an Alleged Extended Sexual Relationship He Had at Age 14 with Kevin Spacey," November 2, 2017, https://www.vulture.com/2017/11/kevin-spacey-alleged-sexual-relationship.html.
32. Regina Borsellino, "How to Make Your Voice Heard in the Workplace (Especially as a Woman or Minority)," October 14, 2021, *the Muse*, https://www.themuse.com/advice/voice-heard-at-work-women-minorities.

Conclusion

1. Teresa Hopke, "White Men Are Feeling Left Out Of Diversity, Equity, & Inclusion. Why Should We Care and What Should We Do?" dated March 30, 2022, Forbes, https://www.forbes.com/sites/teresahopke/2022/03/30/white-men-are-feeling-left-out-of-dei-diversity-equity--inclusion-why-should-we-care-and-what-should-we-do/.

About the Author

Brigitte Gawenda Kimichik, JD

Brigitte, author of *Play Smart – Playground Strategies for Success in a Male-Dominated Workplace*, the second book of THE SANDBOX SERIES, is a passionate advocate for addressing gender discrimination, bullying, sexual harassment and other misconduct in the workplace and beyond. *Play Smart* follows her first book *Play Nice – Playground Rules for Respect in the Workplace,* published in 2019, which she co-authored with JoRayne Tomlinson. Through her blogs and her books, she aims to empower women, educate men, and drive cultural change in and outside of the work environment.

For more of Brigitte's work, please visit thesandboxseries.com. Originally from Germany, Brigitte earned her Abitur from the Gymnasium Osdorf in Hamburg in 1980 before pursuing her studies in the US. She graduated with a BBA from the McCombs School of Business at the University of Texas at Austin in 1983 with Honors, where she was a distinguished member of the Dean's List and the Golden Key Honor Society. Brigitte furthered her education by obtaining a JD in 1986 from the Southern Methodist University Dedman School of Law in Dallas in 1986.

With over thirty years of experience as a commercial real estate finance attorney, Brigitte held partner positions at both Andrews Kurth LLP and Sheinfeld, Maley, and Kay. She also dedicated her time to serving on the boards of Wednesday's Child Benefit Corporation and the alliance board of Genesis Women's Shelter. In 2012, Brigitte was recognized with the Most Powerful and Influential Women of Texas Award from the National Diversity Council.

Retiring in 2015, Brigitte now resides in Dallas, Texas with her husband David. They are proud parents of two accomplished daughters, Nicole and Samantha, who are based in New York City.

To support Brigitte's work and help others discover her books, please consider rating and providing a review of *Play Smart – Playground Strategies for Success in a Male-Dominated Workplace* and her prior book, *Play Nice*, on Amazon, Goodreads, or your social media platforms. For more on her new book *Play Smart*, *Play Nice*, and her related blogs and lessons relating to the subject matter of her books, please visit thesandboxseries.com, sign up for her newsletter, and follow her on Facebook and Instagram.

www.ingramcontent.com/pod-product-compliance
Lightning Source LLC
Chambersburg PA
CBHW060455030426
42337CB00015B/1595